CHOOSING CHILD CARE / A Guide for Parents

Stevanne Auerbach, Ph.D.
Director,
Institute for
Childhood Resources

E. P. DUTTON / NEW YORK

HV
854
.A93

to my daughter
Amy Beth
who shared in the creation
of this book
through our experiences together

Photographic credits:

Illustrations preceding chapters 1, 4, 5, 7, 8, and 10 are copyright © Gary Sinick 1981. Illustrations preceding chapters 2 and 11 are courtesy Iris Rothman. Illustrations preceding chapters 3, 6, and 9 are by the author.

Copyright © 1981 by Stevanne Auerbach

All rights reserved. Printed in the U.S.A.

No part of this publication may be reproduced or transmitted in any form or by any means, electronic or mechanical, including photocopy, recording or any information storage and retrieval system now known or to be invented, without permission in writing from the publisher, except by a reviewer who wishes to quote brief passages in connection with a review written for inclusion in a magazine, newspaper or broadcast.

Published in the United States by E.P. Dutton, Inc.,
2 Park Avenue, New York, N.Y. 10016

Library of Congress Cataloging in Publication Data
Auerbach, Stevanne.
    Choosing child care.
    Bibliography: p.
    1. Day care centers—United States. 2. Education, Preschool—United States. 3. Foster home care—United States. 4. Baby sitters. 5. Children—Management.
I. Title.
HV854.A93 1981   362.7'95   81-9684
AACR2
ISBN: 0-525-93201-1 (cloth) 0-525-93217-8 (paper)

Published simultaneously in Canada by Clarke, Irwin & Company Limited, Toronto and Vancouver

Designed by Nicola Mazzella

10 9 8 7 6 5 4 3 2 1

First Edition

ACKNOWLEDGMENTS

The author wishes to thank the following people who were directly involved in producing this book: *Marsha Bezan, Henry Dakin, Maja Evans, Paul Sibley, Marian Skedgell,* and *Reva Smilkstein.*

The following helped to create this book with their invaluable feedback and advice: *Dr. Millie Almy,* University of California, Berkeley, California; Baby Talk Magazine; *Dr. Joan Bergstrom,* Wheelock College, Boston, Massachusetts; *Dr. Bettye Caldwell,* University of Arkansas, Fayetteville, Arkansas; *Dr. Robert Comas,* University of Alabama; *Jennifer Cross,* "Consumer Action News," San Francisco, California; *Dixie DeVinne,* Stepparents Forum, Montreal, Canada; *Eastern Airlines* Business Woman magazine; *T. Gassenheimer,* Santa Clara Child Care Services, Santa Clara, California; *Dr. David Friedman,* Pediatrician, University of California Medical Center, Los Angeles, California; *Mickey Friedman,* Bookreviews, San Francisco Examiner, San Francisco, California; *Alexander Hamilton,* Parent/Teacher, San Francisco, California; *Dr. James L. Hymes, Jr.,* Berkeley, California; *Genevieve M. Landau,* former editor of Parents Magazine; *Theresa W. Lansburgh,* Maryland Committee for Children; National Committee for Citizens in Education, Network, the paper for parents; *Peggy Pizzo,* Daycare and Early Education magazine.

Acknowledgments | iv

In addition, I acknowledge everyone who participated in the production of first edition: *Carol Brown, Annie Cannon, Marlene Cresci Cohen, Liz Fearon, Linda Freedman, Jim Harrell, Peter Levine, Anne Mason, Howard Montaug, James Rivaldo, Trina Robbins, David Roche, Monique Rothchild, Judith St. Soleil, Patty Siegel, Linda Silver, Helen Valdez,* and *Frank F. Zwilinske.*

I also thank the following people for their contributions in making this book possible: *Surry Blackburn, David Finn, Charles Flewellen, Ralph Kaiser, Gerald LeNoir, Ruth Pancoast,* and *Marvin Silverman.*

Thanks to the many professionals and parents who purchased the privately printed edition from the Parents and Childcare Resources, formerly at the Farwest Laboratory for Education Research and Development in San Francisco.

Contact us at the
Institute for Childhood Resources
1169 Howard Street,
San Francisco, California 94103.

CONTENTS

ACKNOWLEDGMENTS iii
INTRODUCTION ix

1 About Child Care 1
    Parents' Needs 2
    National Trends 2
    Advantages and Disadvantages 3

2 Choosing the Best Plan—A Family Decision 5
    Knowing Yourself 6
    Mothers' Work 7
    Effects of Working on the Parent 7
    Effects of Working on the Child 8
    The Needs of Children 8
    Knowing Your Child 9
    Care of the Baby 12
    Care of the Older Child 12

3 Choosing from What Is Available 15
    What Are the Choices? 16
    About Sitters 17
    About Family Day-Care Homes 18

	About Centers	19
	Other Alternatives	20
4	Getting Ready to Look	25
	Searching Your Community	26
	Talking with Care Givers	27
5	What Is Good Child Care?	31
	What Is a Typical Program?	32
	What Is Quality Child Care?	34
6	Who Are the Child-Care Givers?	37
	Points to Look For	38
	Adult-to-Child Ratios	41
	The Staff	41
	Teen-age Mothers	42
7	Sitters	45
	Why Have a Sitter?	46
	Interviewing a Sitter	46
	Follow-up	47
8	Homes	51
	Gathering Information on the Telephone	52
	What to Look for When You Visit	52
	Follow-up	55
	Checklist	56
9	Centers	59
	Note on Infant Care	63
	After-School Care	63
	The Disabled Child	64
	What to Look For	64
	Checklist	67
10	Looking at the Checklist	69
	The Physical Facility Checklist	72
	The Emotional Climate Checklist	73

The Learning Climate Checklist	75
The Social Climate Checklist	76
Rating the Most Important Checks	77

11 Comparing and Choosing — 81
- *Planning a Workable Budget* — 83
- *Preparing for the First Days and Weeks* — 85
- *Bridging the Gap Between Home and Child Care* — 88
- *Knowing Your Child Is Happy* — 90
- *Connecting with Other Parents* — 90
- *Some Activities for You* — 91
- *Parent Discussion Groups* — 91
- *Sharing Experiences* — 92
- *A Final Word on Child Care and You as a Working Parent* — 95

APPENDIX: RESOURCES — 97
   Child-Care Agencies and Organizations — 97

SUGGESTED EQUIPMENT LIST — 108

FURTHER READING — 111

INDEX — 113

INTRODUCTION

The combination of work and parenthood is a delicate and challenging task. The job requires all the resources, ingenuity, skill, good humor, and strength you can muster.

Millions of parents are working or must return to employment after their children are born, or want to return to school to further their education. Other parents need some time to pursue personal responsibilities. But before they can do any of these things they must see that their child is taken care of while they are away from home.

A few fortunate parents have a friend or relative living nearby to assist them in caring for their child in an informal and inexpensive way. But most parents do not have a relative or friend to assist them. They have no alternative but to look elsewhere in their community to locate child care.

The aim of this guide to child care is to help you find and choose the best child care for your child. It will also help you by shortening the length of time it takes you to find the most suitable arrangement.

The choices vary. You can locate a care giver in your home, in a care giver's home, or in a child-care center. However, finding a good and convenient sitter, home, or center is definitely not easy. Good child-care programs usually have long waiting lists and may be inconvenient to reach from your home or cost more than you can afford, or they may not offer the kind of care you want. Most communities fall short of providing enough good child care to meet the demand.

All parents in search of child care seem to want the same thing—a secure place that will provide care, learning opportunities, and values that do not conflict with their own point of view. They seek a safe, attractive place staffed with sensitive and caring adults, who have at hand an ample and varied supply of teaching materials, toys, and sturdy, practical equipment. They would like a sliding scale of fees based on ability to pay.

For many parents the search for child care is only one of several difficult personal and family problems. Eager to solve at least one problem as soon as possible, they may settle for the first available child-care arrangement. One young mother told me how she had met a woman at the laundromat who said she would take care of the child. The woman had not had any recent child-care experience, but she had just lost her husband and thought she would enjoy having some young person to look after. The mother was anxious to begin a new job and gave the care of her fifteen-month-old child to the woman. The first few days the mother called during the day and everything seemed all right. But when she arrived at the end of the day to pick up her baby, she noticed the baby's pants were wet and the baby was cranky and irritable long into the evening. One day deciding to check on the situation, she dropped by and found the woman watching soap operas with the child parked in a playpen—much to the young mother's dismay.

Because an unsatisfactory child-care arrangement can become as great an emotional problem and energy drain as finding the child care in the first place, it is well worth the time and effort to make a thorough investigation before you decide. The quick solution is no solution if your peace of mind suffers.

Finding the situation where you and your child will be happy may take weeks of searching and visiting. Often, finding child care can be as complicated and stressful as finding a new place to live.

The information in this guide will assist you in selecting the best possible child-care services with the least amount of time and effort. Included are detailed checklists giving specific points to look for in each of the places you visit. I've also indicated the kind of realistic questions you should ask at different stages of your search.

The information and suggestions given should help to reduce your feelings of uncertainty in selecting a child-care situation. However, only you can make the final decision, based on the personal needs of both you and your child.

I vividly recall the experiences I had when my daughter was a baby and I had to return to work. The balancing act between home and work was never easy, yet we learn from our experiences. I want to share these experiences with you to help you to find the best child care available in your community.

STEVANNE AUERBACH

1 / About Child Care

PARENTS' NEEDS

During an extensive study of child care, I interviewed hundreds of parents of all economic and ethnic groups who used family day-care homes and centers. Mothers revealed to me in their own language (through translators, if they did not speak English) some of their concerns related to child care. I learned that all of these parents needed good reliable child care in order to continue working or going to school.

One parent, a nurse, had had a problem finding child care at night. She finally made arrangements with a neighbor, whose child was about the same age as her own. The neighbor took care of her child evenings in exchange for her care of the neighbor's child on the weekends.

Another mother, who was going to college, was worried that she would not be able to continue school because the child-care arrangements that she had depended on for some time had broken down. She eventually located a service near the campus and, fortunately, was able to finish school.

For still another parent, a father who had just obtained custody of two young boys (ages six and seven), the problem of after-school care was critical. The boys needed supervision until he came home from work. He was fortunate to find a private service which provided after-school care. In each of the above cases, the parent's needs and solutions related to their differing work schedules and individual situations.

NATIONAL TRENDS

The use of child-care services is increasing throughout the United States. During World War II, child-care services were plentiful, but they declined in the immediate postwar years. Now with inflation, it has become necessary for more mothers to return to work. More than one half of the mothers with preschool children are in the work force. Currently, 13 million children under the age of fourteen require some form of child care, including school, for ten hours or more each day. In 1980, 900,000 places were available for children in licensed centers and 300,000 places in licensed homes. Obviously not enough places are available to care for all the children who need it.

The number of working mothers increased by seventy-nine percent since 1970, or by one in every five families. Seventeen percent of all families are headed by a single mother and two percent by a single father.

ADVANTAGES AND DISADVANTAGES

Research shows that early child care has many benefits for the child. Children gain in independence; they learn to read sooner and develop other academic skills; they converse more easily with others; they have a better idea of individual sex roles.

One mother reported that her child, who whined and complained at home about not liking many foods, found that he enjoyed the variety of foods offered at the child-care program. Another mother, who was concerned about her child learning to read, found that the patience with which the care giver talked to the child and read books to him prepared him for recognizing words.

Children who have the opportunity to play and interact with other children grow in their ability to get along with others. They also learn a number of games and activities that they may not have the opportunity to learn otherwise. As children interact and play with others, they grow in self-esteem and confidence.

Children of divorced parents, who frequently do not see the father, benefit from interaction with the males who are involved in child-care services.

One disadvantage that is frequently mentioned is that child care will break up the family. In fact, the opposite may be true—the lack of support services, such as child care, results in unnecessary strain for the parents in the early years and may lead to divorce.

Parents report that, as a result of having child care available, their own situations improved. They felt much better about their ability to care for and support their families. One mother who felt particularly stressed and was not able to cope with some of her personal needs, saw that after she began to utilize child-care services, she functioned better in both her personal life and her part-time job.

Parents often find child care essential to their economic well-being. Studies show that the welfare rolls are reduced and the average income is raised with the parents' higher earning power, and the capability of the children increases. Many mothers told me repeatedly that after finding child care they were able to get off welfare and enjoy the many opportunities that opened to them for training and job placement. Recently divorced mothers find that they could not maintain themselves or their families without the aid of child care.

Other advantages for the parents include the chance to talk to other parents about their children's needs and to expand their own social relationships. Many mothers mentioned the advantages of the discussion groups provided by the center. Still others were able to develop a parent cooperative for weekends or form a network of sitters. Often, parents feel less isolated than previously.

Child care provides for other essential needs outside of the obvious ones. One mother, a lawyer, told me that her son, age four, had changed from being a shy and introverted child to one with enthusiasm and joy as a result of being in a day-care group. He was proud of each day's accomplishments and his mother knew that while she was preparing herself for further responsibilities her son was also.

A divorced father told me that his children were better able to cope with the changes in their lives because of the encounters they had at the child-care center with other children of divorced parents. The father also gained the comfort of talking over issues regarding the child-care center with parents in a similar situation. Particularly, he was relieved when his daughter, age three, appeared less sad after she joined the program. By meeting other children and expressing herself openly, she became a more secure and happier child.

Many varieties of child-care services exist now, and the situation is improving as the types and amount of services provided increase to meet the demands of the families. Child care is often available to some employees through union activities or employer-supported activities.

Perhaps in the near future, support groups will pool their energies to improve at the national level the planning and implementation of child-care services. In the meantime, it is the parent who has the responsibility and the challenge of finding the best services possible.

2 / Choosing the Best Plan— A Family Decision

KNOWING YOURSELF

You are now a parent or soon will be one. You are thinking about combining work or school with your family life. If you are going to be away from your child at any time of the day or night, you will need child care. What kind you choose will depend on where you live and what you can spend, on the number of available spaces, the number of families who want the same services, and on your own insistence on obtaining those services. You probably have many other questions. For example:

"What effects will working have on my child and me?"
"How much of my earnings will be left after child-care and other work-related expenses?"
"How much will I have to participate and become involved in a child-care program?"
"How will illness—either of my child or myself—affect my employment?"

These are just some of the concerns expressed by parents who are considering working or who have been working. There are no easy answers to these questions, especially since every parent has special needs, motivations, desires, and problems.

A friend or neighbor who has been able to look after your child may no longer be able to do so. Perhaps you are recently divorced and must return to work, or you want to complete your education. Whether or not you are employed, you may need to have time to take care of certain other personal interests.

Whatever you are doing now or want to do is important to you as a person. You may be discovering new talents and abilities or may be seeking ways to gain new skills. Perhaps you worked before your child was born and now want to update your skills. You may want to prepare yourself for a future opportunity.

Knowing what you want and need is very important. Child-care services will make a big difference in giving you the chance to earn, to go to school or respond to other needs, and to provide important personal advantages for your child at the same time.

MOTHERS' WORK

According to recent estimates, the American mother with two children devotes at least 100 hours a week to the family, or 5,200 hours a year. If she were paid, it has been estimated by the Harvard Insurance Group that her salary would be a minimum of $10,400 a year. Other estimates by attorney Michael Minton of Chicago value her services at $40,000 a year.

When one realizes the many services a woman performs for her family, it is evident that her value to that family is very high. Though there is an increase in the number of men who are sharing the responsibilities of the home, the main responsibility still rests with the mother. Even after she is working, either part-time or full-time, many of these responsibilities remain hers. For her continued well-being and that of her family, it is important for parents to discuss ways to share responsibilities for the home, the children, and each other. Some of the responsibilities that should be considered are: cleaning, shopping, medical appointments, sewing, dry cleaning, laundry, social commitments, and home repairs. If you are a single parent, you may be able to share some of these responsibilities with another single parent who lives nearby.

EFFECTS OF WORKING ON THE PARENT

During a study conducted of child-care services and parents' needs, a teacher I spoke to said that she was very unhappy while staying home during the first few months after her child was born. She needed to earn money and was unable to use the skills for which she was trained. She felt somehow that flexible hours or sharing a job with another teacher would have allowed her to be a satisfied parent at home and also be productive outside the home, as the additional income was sorely needed.

Another woman who was divorced when her child was three years old found that returning to work was an absolute necessity. She found a well-paying secretarial job and studied to brush up on her skills in accounting. Now she works as a bookkeeper. A child-care arrangement allowed her to improve her life and the life of her child. Most working mothers, if they find the right situation for their child, report their family life becomes more stable, productive, and dependable.

Many divorced mothers told me how much better they felt about themselves, their strengths and abilities, and their children's ability to cope with changes, after they had successfully solved the problems of finding a job and a satisfactory child-care situation.

EFFECTS OF WORKING ON THE CHILD

There is no reason to worry that being away from your child during the day will harm the child if you first take steps to prepare the child and yourself for the change. You will have to arrange meals, housecleaning, and your personal needs carefully around the more limited time you will have. You also will want to set aside time each day to be with your child to talk, play, read, and share with each other.

Your children want to participate and assist you as you take on new responsibilities if you allow them to do so. Carefully teach them to pick up their toys, clothing, and other personal belongings. Children can help to set and clear the table, and help with chores around the house, such as dusting and other kinds of light housekeeping. Children respond to the challenge of responsibility, especially if they understand the importance of their contribution to the family.

THE NEEDS OF CHILDREN

Children vary greatly individually but in general have certain growth patterns. The child is most dependent up to two-and-a-half years of age and needs a stable individual to provide reassurance and continuity in care. But if the child is two or more, he also needs freedom to move around and be active, so that the best program for him at that age balances flexibility with firmness. At age three, when children are taking the first steps toward establishing their own individuality, it is important for them to be in a situation that allows them free expression within definable limits, particularly in regard to attitudes toward sex, play, activities, and the use of equipment.

Tommy, for example, was an only child and at the age of one and a half he needed a completely secure and stable situation. His mother found a neighborhood program within a few blocks of their

Choosing the Best Plan | 9

home where she was able to give him the comfortable feeling that he was close to home and in familiar surroundings. As Jane developed, on the other hand, she needed to be with other children who were in her age range, two or two and a half, and to have more exciting activities while her mother was busy with the new baby. The half-day program she attended fitted her needs exactly. She was able to make friends, gain social skills, and find many new outlets for her energy. Three-year-old Johnny expressed the need to play with boys his own age. The child-care center near his home was the perfect solution for him. Other children, at four or four and a half, develop new skills and adapt better to school the following year if they have had at least a half day of child care. Almost all children who have attended a nursery school or a child-care center find adjustment to kindergarten or first grade much easier.

Specifically, benefits to the child in a child-care situation are in the early stimulation that contributes to faster growth and development. Children who would be otherwise alone for the better part of the day find that playing with other children builds their self confidence and their ability to relate to others. Most children benefit from the opportunity to meet and be with children from different backgrounds. Many mothers reported to me that their children learned many useful skills.

KNOWING YOUR CHILD

The first step in thinking about your child's needs is to think about your child's personality and how he responds to other children or adults. Is your child ready to cope with the change from home to child care at this time? If not, you will want to assist your child in making the transition by providing opportunities to sleep away at a relative's home or at the home of a friend, or by making arrangements with a sitter your child knows. If your child is two years old or older, teach the child self-help skills, such as tying his shoes and putting on and taking off his own clothes.

How would you describe your child? If your child is quiet, it would be best to start with a program that will not push children to enter into too many activities. If your child is outgoing and self-confident, a child-care center that is more active and perhaps with a broader program would give him or her a variety of new friends. If your child is not toilet trained, he or she will feel more comfortable if personal attention can easily be obtained. If your child has a special health problem, a child-care center can sometimes be found to meet those special needs.

Certainly, your child needs contact with adults other than yourself before he attends a child-care center. He needs to feel comfortable with other adults and have the experience and confidence that once you leave him you will come back to him. Children learn to adapt to different situations at different rates. You will need to be sensitive to your child's reactions. You can help your child to respond favorably to new people by talking to him about visitors before they come to your home or about people he will go to see. The more experience the child has of being away from you, the more easily he will adapt to the child-care situation. The more your child feels good about him or herself, the more the child will enjoy contact with other children.

If you take pains to consider the special needs of your child, his or her unique personality and responses, your chances of working out a satisfactory arrangement are greater. It is important to know the styles and personalities of the other children to know if your child will fit in with the group.

For those children who will need some extra time to make the transition from home to child care, an individual sitter or a family day-care home with only a few children is usually a good first step. Other children who have had many chances to be away from their parents can function well in larger groups. They would find it challenging and would enjoy the wider number of activities offered by a large center.

As you visit each place, ask yourself:

1. How much individual attention does my child need?
2. Will my child be comfortable and secure in this place?
3. Who are the adults and how will they respond to my child?
4. How will my child fit into this group of children?
5. How much does this place feel like home?
6. What will be expected of me?
7. What are the staff attitudes about child rearing?

These questions are among those on the checklists given in chapter 10 on what to look for at each place you visit.

Children usually adjust well when the philosophy and methods of their child-care program do not contrast too sharply with what their parents do at home. Of course, your child will learn some new attitudes and pick up mannerisms of other children and adults in the center or home. Don't worry: these aren't necessarily permanent. Children grow and change rapidly.

You usually know when you walk into a place whether you like it or not. It has to do with your philosophy and the kinds of values you feel are most important. One mother reported to me that as soon as she walked into one child-care situation, she got an immediate sense of well-being and nurturing. The place was clean, bright, and comfortable. The adults were warm and made her feel welcome, the children were happy and laughing. She had already visited several places. Elsewhere she had found that there weren't enough toys, or the place was disorganized, or there wasn't a convincing sense of security. She knew that this last place was the right place for her child.

You may want to consider a center or home where there is an emphasis on developing cultural identity and pride. Such cultural values will help to enhance your child's sense of security, confidence, and self-respect. One of the women I interviewed, Mrs. Rodriguez, felt strongly about her cultural heritage. Wanting to preserve that for her children, she searched for a bilingual center that would teach her children English, yet would allow and encourage them to feel proud about their cultural background and language. She found such a place a few blocks away after talking to many parents in her neighborhood.

Children sense it if you like and feel comfortable in the place you're sending them to. But you shouldn't choose a center simply because it matches your notions of child care. Just note what your reaction is.

You know your child best. Consider your child's and your own feelings about the place, the adults, and the other children. Most of all, trust your own feelings as to whether the staff has a warm, personal interest in you and your child.

CARE OF THE BABY

A great deal of controversy has centered on the appropriate age for leaving a child at a secondary home location. Most mothers find that adjustments are much easier when the child is at least six months old or older. Whatever the age, the child should have a consistent caretaker. A baby is particularly sensitive and needs a great deal of loving, affectionate care. For infant care, family day-care homes where one individual is in charge are the best choice. If the mother feels comfortable with the arrangement and the baby is doing well, there should be no cause for concern.

Working Mother magazine, in the November 1979 issue, reported that thirty percent of the women responding to a questionnaire had returned to their jobs when their children were less than six months old. They had been able to arrange for child care by sitters or relatives in or near their home.

CARE OF THE OLDER CHILD

A mother's return to work involves all members of the family, including the children, in a family decision. You can prepare the children for separation by simple overnights at other homes, or by leaving them with other people, such as relatives, sitters, and friends, for short periods of time. You will come to learn that other adults can care for your children, and the children will learn that you come back for them.

By the age of four, a child should be able to care for himself to a certain extent. For example, he should be able to brush his teeth, comb his hair, dress and undress, put on his shoes, go to the bathroom, wash his hands, possibly tell time, and match colors, sizes, and shapes. Teaching these skills is one of the responsibilities parents have in educating their own children in self-help skills. Talk to your children about books and ideas, take trips with them to nearby places, answer their questions, and also make sure they can understand and follow directions. These are all good ways to prepare them to enjoy and get the most out of their time away from you.

If you are returning to work, you will want to encourage your child to learn other skills, such as putting away his toys, setting the table, using a fork and knife, and pouring from a container. As children learn these self-help skills, they get a sense of accomplishment and heightened self-esteem.

The older child can take responsibility for keeping the room straight, and dusting, watering plants, tending the garden, and feeding pets. If the mother is going to work, she cannot handle all the responsibilities of the home. The more the family works together, the better it is for everyone.

When the time for separation comes, be direct and reassuring with your child. You are going away and you will return: this can be done without deception, games, or emotional trauma:

> *Susie, Mommy will be going back to work and you are going to have time to play with other children at a special place. Mrs. Smith is a person who enjoys taking care of children, and we have talked about having you stay with her while Mommy is at work. I'm sure you will like her very much and will enjoy being with other children. We will be going to Mrs. Smith's in a couple of days and I wanted you to know about it. We will visit the office tomorrow so you will know where Mommy is going to work, and Mrs. Smith will always be able to reach me there by telephone so you can talk to me any time you need to. I will take you there in the morning and when I finish work I will pick you up in the afternoon.*

Your child will know by your tone of voice and your attitude what to expect from this new situation, so it is important to have a positive attitude when you talk about it. Under no circumstances should you leave your child without telling him what will be happening to him. If the child is well prepared the experience has a better chance of becoming a happy one.

Children can cope with new experiences if they are prepared physically and emotionally. A simple rule is: The better your child is prepared, the more he will benefit from the experience.

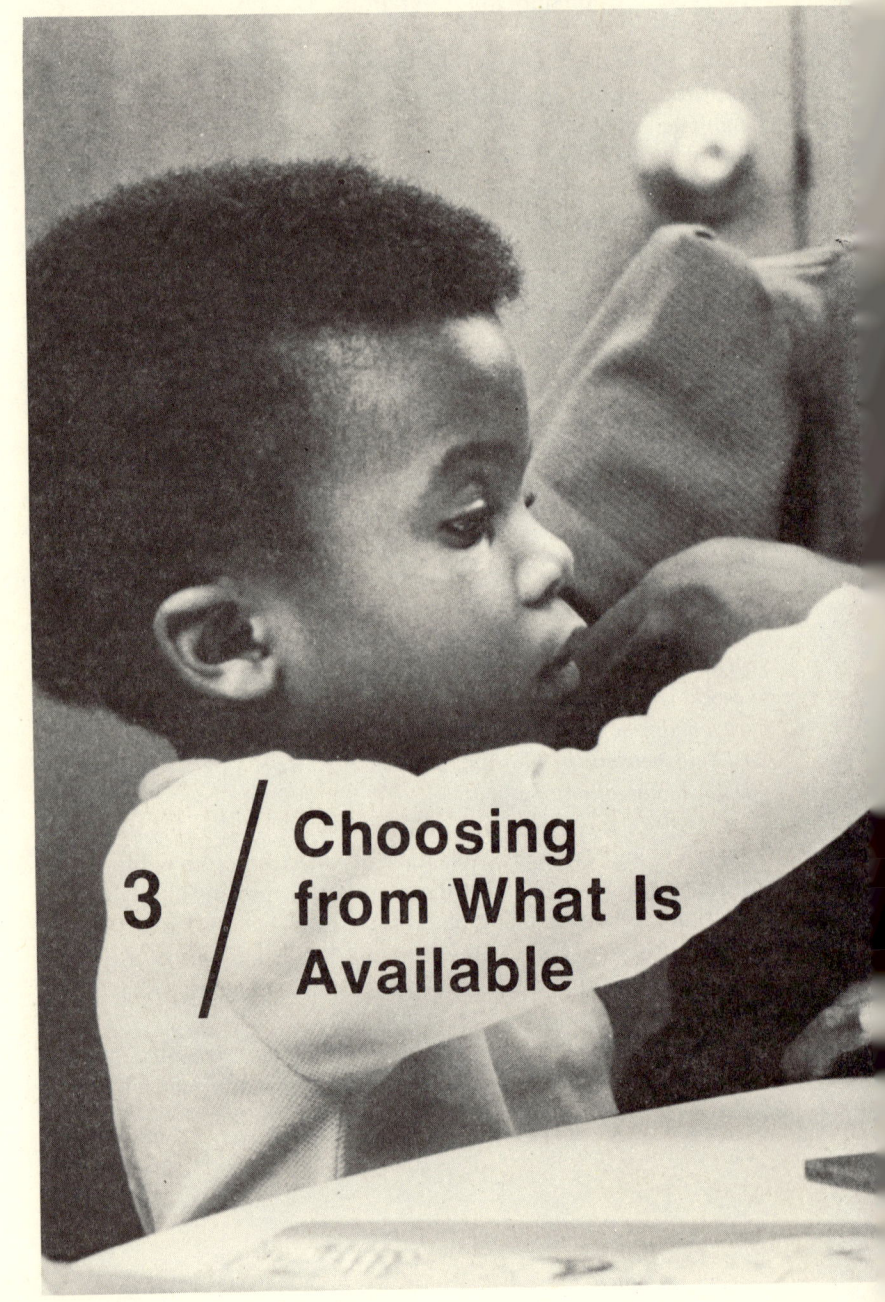

3 / Choosing from What Is Available

WHAT ARE THE CHOICES?

Possible child-care arrangements include:

1. An individual sitter (in your home or the sitter's home).
2. A group family day-care home.
3. A child-care center.

Before discussing in detail each type of program, let us review some of the pros and cons of individual sitters, family day-care homes, and child-care centers. You will want *consistent-accessible-reliable-affordable* services no matter which type you eventually choose.

Consistent. Will this be someone or someplace you can count on to take good care of your child, day after day, for an extended period of time?

Accessible. Will this be someone or someplace you can get to without too much difficulty in terms of time, distance, and expense? Do the hours coincide with your schedule?

Reliable. Will you be able to trust the sitter or child-care staff with your child's safety and well-being? Will they be *where* you need them *when* you need them?

Affordable. Will this be someone or someplace that will charge you no more than what you can reasonably manage within your budget?

The cost of child care varies from fifty cents an hour to $3.00 or more an hour, from $600 a year to about $5,500. The average cost tends to be close to $1.00 an hour or $2,050 a year.

The money received is spent on staff salaries, food, staff training, medical services, rent, and equipment. The costs vary, depending on the number of adults per child.

In some state-sponsored programs child care can be free for some, or it can be very expensive, depending on your situation and the number and ages of your children. The amount you have to pay does not always indicate the quality of the program. Don't assume that the more expensive program is the better one. Be sure to investigate such low-cost or free options as parent cooperatives and play groups. In this chapter there is information on these types of child

Choosing from What Is Available | 17

care and you will find further references on child care in the Appendix.

ABOUT SITTERS

A sitter is an individual who is hired to care for your child in your home or in the sitter's home during the day or evening. Sitters usually are paid by the hour or week. Federal law requires that sitters who work more than ninety hours a month receive the current minimum wage of $3.25 per hour.

Sitters can be an expensive, but convenient, choice. If you have more than two young children, you may wish to hire a sitter so the children can stay together in their own home. This would also save you extra transportation and other costs. But it is difficult to locate a good sitter who has had training and experience with young children and is actually looking for a job.

To find a person who is kind and gentle and knows how and when to respond to your child in a positive and interested way is not easy. People who are well qualified for this work are in high demand and earn high salaries. Sometimes, on a part-time basis, you may be able to obtain the services of an elderly person, a retired teacher, a part-time student, or a relative. Or you may join with two other parents to hire someone who would care for all the children in one of your homes.

If the sitter will be working without supervision in your home, you must be very cautious. You will want to check references, previous experience, and the personality traits of the person you are considering. An employment agency can assist you in this regard, although agencies are not as careful in their screening of people as you must be. Before an agency sends a prospective sitter to your home for the first interview, get as much information as possible from the agency representative in your initial telephone conversation to avoid wasting time.

Your child usually is unable to tell you how he or she feels about the prospective sitter. Note your child's responses to the person and how the person responds to your child. Once you have hired someone, make sure that the sitter discusses your child's progress at the end of the day and describes any difficulties encountered. Taking time is critical in establishing a good relationship with a sitter.

ABOUT FAMILY DAY-CARE HOMES

Family day care is provided in homes set up to care for from two to twelve children. Such a home setting is the most common type of child care outside the home. The providers of family day-care homes have modified their homes to fit the needs of a small group of infants, preschoolers, or school-age children. The number of children in the home varies, although state laws typically require that no more than six children under six, including the provider's own children, or only two children, if under two, be cared for in the home at one time.

There are two basic kinds of family day-care homes, small and large. A small home cares for six or fewer children, from infants through children of six years of age. A larger home can care for up to twelve children and the federal interagency guidelines recommend that two adults be present.

Regulations for family day-care homes vary from state to state. In general, licensing regulations of these homes are aimed at safeguarding the child and don't necessarily relate to the educational or social aspects of the program. Licensing homes does give you some protection but does not guarantee quality.

State, city, or county licensing most often assures you that the home meets certain minimum standards of health and safety. Some regulations require personal qualifications on the part of the provider. Nevertheless, a license does not assure you that the services provided will be satisfactory to you or your child. Sometimes a home is not licensed because the regulations may require physical alterations in the house that the provider cannot make. Ask to see the license and note the last time it was certified by a visit from the licensing agency. If the place is not licensed, ask why.

Be very careful if you must consider an unlicensed place. The state and local standards have been set up to protect the best interests of children with the highest quality possible, and not having a license may indicate a serious deficiency not immediately apparent. A specific checklist of what to look for in a family day-care home is included in this book (see chapter 8).

A family day-care home has many advantages. Most day-care homes are run by women who have raised or are raising their own children and have experience with and affection for children.

If your child is already in kindergarten or the primary grades, he or she may be cared for and supervised before and after school in such a home. If you have a preschooler the child may be in a group with other two-to-four-year-olds.

The family home is usually best for a very young child or infant because of the close personal attention from the adults in charge. For the child who needs the warmth and the closeness of a small group of children, a family day-care home may be the best choice. Also, a home may be willing to care for a moderately ill child, while a larger center might exclude the child, forcing you to stay at home and lose a day of work or classes. Another advantage is that it is easy for an older child to come there after school if it is near the child's home.

The disadvantages of a family day-care home include the following:

1. The children do not always have the variety of supervision they would have by the larger staff in a center.
2. The provider may not be able to offer the variety of activities or equipment provided by a center.
3. The children may spend too much time watching television.
4. If the provider becomes ill, you may have to make other child-care arrangements on short notice.
5. Children in a single-family day-care home may lack the contact with the variety of adults they would meet at a larger center.

ABOUT CENTERS

Centers provide child care for groups of from 10 to 100 children. Some centers offer child care for both infants and preschoolers, but most provide care for preschoolers only. Some others offer after-school care also.

Centers are located in schools, churches, recreation centers, or in separate buildings. They usually have outdoor play space or a park nearby. They may provide breakfast and lunch as well as midmorning and midafternoon snacks. Naps and rest times are balanced with play and educational opportunities.

The children usually have a wider variety of activities, materials, and play equipment than they would find in a family day-care home. The staff are usually trained and knowledgeable. The hours the center is open coincide with most parents' work schedules. Although centers may vary according to the staff, the sponsor, and the parents involved, most offer very reliable care.

Centers have certain disadvantages: they may be expensive, or charge more than you can afford, or be difficult to reach from where you live. They may have too many children and not be able to give each child the individual attention he may need. They also may not be able to care for more than one child from a family.

If your work hours are not during the day, you may have to choose a home or a sitter willing to provide evening care. The problem of finding child care during off-hours is especially acute for nurses and other hospital workers who have evening or night shifts. To meet their needs, some institutions offer child-care services nearby. Perhaps the organization that hired you could provide or assist you in finding child care. Also, a number of employees can band together to press for better child-care services from their employer. You might want to join a group of other persons who are interested in and advocate better child-care services.

OTHER ALTERNATIVES

Other arrangements for child care exist and are worth considering. However, most of the alternatives require your personal involvement and attention on an ongoing basis to make them work. If you can balance the time and conditions of participation with your other responsibilities, you could have an excellent arrangement.

A *play group* is one alternative. It is an informal cooperative operated and organized entirely by parents.

Choosing from What Is Available | 21

A play group is often the only inexpensive child care available for infants and toddlers. The groups may operate on a rotating-home basis, which works well if no more than five children are in the group, and they are together for only a few hours each day. Sometimes a play group is formed when one parent exchanges child care with one other person once a week. Other parents and children come into the play group gradually.

Parents have organized play groups that provide care for as many as twenty children. Typically the parents hire a teacher to work with each of the parents. The teacher provides skill, direction, and continuity to the group. If arrangements can be made for the group to meet with the teacher in the same place each day, services can be provided for more hours to more children. Hiring a regular teacher is often essential to large play-group management.

One disadvantage of play groups is the time and responsibility involved in their operation. If you have more than one child and must place your children in different groups because of their ages, scheduling play-group time to coordinate with your work can quickly become complicated. Play-group days are often disrupted when parents can't show up as scheduled, and the whole group must readjust immediately. Problems such as deciding who is going to be responsible for what can slow down group meetings. Only if the parents have organizational abilities and sufficient time will a play group keep running smoothly.

The other major problem with play groups is that sometimes the parents are at a loss for what to do with the children during play-group time. By sharing skills and creative energy, parents can provide a flow of good activities for young children during the day and learn the best ways to handle discipline. A play group means parents learning and working together.

Some play groups deal with these various problems successfully. By visiting an established play group, you can get an idea of whether it will be suitable for you. Arrange to attend one of the group's meetings for more direct information, a feeling about how it operates, and to find out what the other parents are like. For the steps necessary to begin organizing a play group, we suggest you read *The Playgroup Handbook* listed in Further Reading.

Part-day programs for preschoolers are a good alternative for children ages two to four and they are readily available. Half-day programs run either mornings or afternoons. They vary in cost depending on the sponsoring group. Some are parent cooperatives with hired teachers and parents assisting in providing the program. Usually the staff is professional.

For many years half-day programs have been recognized for the positive contributions they make to the child's early development. They have been the most widespread form of out-of-the-home child care and early education experience. Now, in response to the needs of working parents, some half-day programs have been extended to full-day operation.

One of the most noteworthy of the part-day nursery school programs is Head Start, which is supported by the federal government. The Head Start program gives children the opportunity to have an early education which many parents normally cannot afford. Unfortunately, too few of these federally-funded half-day programs are available to provide a child-care alternative for most of the low-income working parents who want to work part or full time.

Often the part-day preschool is the only program around with space available. You may be able to find someone to pick up your child at the school and to baby-sit for the remaining hours each day at your home or theirs. It is more worrisome to have your child in several different places during the day than having him or her in one safe, secure place. However, this arrangement can work if the segments of your child's day are scheduled carefully.

Pooling your resources is another alternative. You may be able to join with another parent on a regular basis and work out an economical and effective arrangement. Together, you can afford to hire the kind of sitter you couldn't afford to hire individually. If an age difference keeps your children from being accepted at the same place of child care, you can create your own family day-care home situation with another parent by employing a sitter to come into one of your homes.

Baby-sitting co-ops are also a good arrangement. They are organized through large food co-ops, colleges or universities, large companies, and community organizations. Often they only emphasize occasional exchanges of services, giving you a list of students or other persons to choose from. Frequently it is hard to get a sitting exchange going on a regular basis unless one person is in overall charge or unless the responsibility rotates according to an agreed-upon schedule.

A *communal living arrangement* is yet another alternative if you and others agree to live together to share child care. Living together can be a complicated problem or a simple solution, depending on the people involved. If you are well-matched and are willing to cooperate and share responsibilities, it will work out all around. The important thing is, you need to be able to talk freely to the person or persons with whom you will be sharing your child's care.

Family or friends may occasionally have the time and commitment to raise your children as their own. More often, relatives and friends offer only limited and sporadic help.

4 / Getting Ready to Look

Looking at your needs and the needs of your child is the first step in choosing child care. The next step is searching among the various arrangements possible. Use the checklists in chapter 10 to help you decide. The choice you make will affect you, your work, and your child.

The feelings you have about the place and the people in it are very important, but the feelings your child will have once in the situation are even more important. Adults can change jobs, classes, or situations more easily than children. If you select carefully, making sure that your child's overall needs are met, the experience will be rewarding and positive for everyone.

SEARCHING YOUR COMMUNITY

Your first step in arranging child care is to explore the options available in your community. Set aside a few hours one morning to make some preliminary telephone calls. You can get a lot of information over the phone without having to make a commitment.

To prepare for your morning phone calls, list phone numbers on a sheet of paper. In some lucky communities, one phone call to a child-care information and referral service will give you a lot of assistance. Quite often, such a referral service has a staff on hand five days a week answering parents' telephone inquiries about where to find child care. Some have a "Switchboard" or referral service to assist parents in setting up alternatives such as play groups and small preschools. The referral service will give you current information on available centers, day-care homes and co-op arrangements.

In most localities a state or county office has a listing of licensed family day-care homes in your area. Since they may be unable to give you the list the same day you call, call them a few days before you plan to make your morning phone calls. To reach the government department that provides this service consult your telephone directory. Look under the Department of Education, Social Services, the Office of Children's Services, or the Health Department. In some places, you can get a list of all licensed centers or homes in your area by calling the state or county health or education department responsible for the licensing programs (see the Appendix for a list).

Other sources from which to gather phone numbers of possible child-care services are newspapers, school placement offices, bulletin boards, the offices of pediatricians, stores that sell children's products, community centers, and under "Nursery Schools" in the Yellow Pages. Your particular pediatrician might know of some good child-care arrangement in your area. It's worth a call to ask.

Sitters and family day-care homes often advertise in newspapers, so get both the large dailies and the smaller local weeklies. These people also advertise in local laundromats and on supermarket bulletin boards, so be sure to look there. However, many excellent sitters or informal day-care homes rely on word of mouth and don't bother to advertise. Ask everyone you meet if they know of any good child-care arrangements. Through a conversation in the park one day, one mother found an excellent sitter who lived right across the street from her. Another informal conversation between two parents at the supermarket checkout counter led them onto the topic of sitters. One parent found the perfect sitter through the chance referral made by the other parent.

Don't settle for the first person you find, or the place that's nearest at hand, even if appearances seem perfect. Check several situations so you can be certain you have found the best arrangement and so you will have possible alternatives if you need them later.

The information you gather on sitters, centers, homes, and informal alternatives may quickly become overwhelming and confusing. Keep all information in a notebook and make lists of phone numbers for each type of situation—sitters, homes, centers, and any other alternative arrangements you find. Organize the information in your notebook by location, cost, and type of service. Now you are ready to take the next step—obtaining specific information on each situation.

TALKING WITH CARE GIVERS

When you call the person or place, you are seeking detailed information. Although some items are better to cover while you are visiting, a lot of preliminary screening can be done over the phone. You will know to go no further if the person you are talking to does not want you to visit, or is unwilling to answer your questions, or has a brusque manner which is not due to temporarily being tired or ill.

Record the information you get in the notebook you are compiling. Your first conversation might go like this:

> "Hello. My name is _____. I have a job with _____ and have a young child who is _____ years old. I am looking for child care and would like to know if you have space in your program. . . . Do you have time to talk about it now? . . . Do you have an application form and can you send it please? Thank you very much."

You may still want to continue with your questions even if there are no openings, if the person has the time, and you may keep this information for a possible opening later. Or the person may ask you to call back when it is more convenient to talk with you.

Here are some questions you may ask on the phone before you decide to visit:

1. Do you have a current license? Who licenses you? (If there is no license, find out why.)
2. How many children are you taking care of?
3. How many adults work there?
4. What hours are you open? When can the children come and when is pickup time?
5. How much do you charge? Do you have a sliding-fee scale?
6. Would you describe the building? Program? Activities? What is a typical schedule of the children's day?
7. Do you provide any special services, such as transportation? Health care? Trips?
8. What are the meals like and who prepares them?
9. Who will be with my child? (If this is not already apparent.)
10. How does the sitter or center handle *individual differences* in children (energy levels, interest, skills, and so forth)?
11. What are the special skills you have? Where did you get your training to work with children?
12. Can I talk with other parents who use your program?

Getting Ready to Look | 29

13. What arrangements are made in emergencies such as an illness to care for the children?

If your questions have been answered to your satisfaction, arrange a date and time to visit when can you meet the person who will have the most contact with your child and when the children will be involved in their usual activities. If a visit is not in order, thank the person for his or her time and continue through your list.

Sometimes the waiting list is very long, especially for a good program. This may be discouraging. If the program is what you want, however, it may be advisable to place your name on the list for the future. Sometimes a space will open up just when you are ready for a change anyway. A busy director or family day-care-home provider might discourage you from visiting until there actually is room in the program for your child. But if the program sounds excellent and it is convenient and possible to visit to find out what it is like, do so. Then you'll be more certain about using the service later on.

5 / What Is Good Child Care?

WHAT IS A TYPICAL PROGRAM?

A good program for children balances active pursuits with restful interludes, alone, or as part of a large or small group. Depending on the staff and the ages of children, the basic elements of the program include: talking and sharing, indoor and outdoor play, arts and crafts, reading stories, and special projects. A program for preschoolers will include learning numbers, puzzles, games, music, cooking, and everyday living routines that children need to learn and gain skills in. Meals and snacks, naps, and clean-up time are part of most programs.

The quality of the staff is critically important to the effectiveness of the child-care service. The equipment and facilities will vary, the food served will differ, but the most important aspects are who the adults are and how they relate to the children.

The following is a typical day's program in a structured setting, such as a family day-care home or a child-care center. The specifics will vary from place to place. A sitter would arrange her own schedule of activities.

Morning

7:00– 9:15	Free play, inside and out
9:15– 9:30	Cleanup and bathroom
9:30–10:00	Group time, sharing and music
10:00–11:00	Various indoor activities, learning centers, and projects
11:00–11:30	Outdoor play
11:30–12:00	Story time and bathroom (cleanup and rest period)

Afternoon

12:00–12:30	Lunch
12:30– 2:30	Nap
2:30– 3:30	Get-up time and snack time
3:00– 3:45	Arts and crafts, free play
3:45– 4:00	Cleanup
4:00– 5:00	Outdoor play
5:00– 6:00	Quiet activities

On arriving, the children are greeted by the staff and made to feel welcome. They put their coats or sweaters in the storage unit; then, depending on the hour, they may have breakfast with the other children. Some programs give parents menus of the food to be served during the week so that they can plan their own menus accordingly.

The first session includes any number of activities geared to the age level and interests of the children. This is a time when some children will be working on specific skills, by learning through doing. Typical activities of this nature are storytelling, cutting out pictures, assembling puzzles, listening to records, dramatic play, growing things, using art materials, making things, playing with blocks, learning shapes, experimenting with colors, and discovering movement through exercise or dance. Later, the children have time to go outdoors and play; sand, water, blocks, tricycles, and other toys make this time challenging and fun.

When the children return indoors for cleanup and rest before lunch, there may be music to listen to or quiet songs and stories. Lunchtime is always a major event and is an enjoyable time for everyone. Sometimes the children help to prepare the food. Making salad, Jell-O, cookies, or preparing fruits and vegetables are activities children enjoy.

Naps after lunch are vital to the children's well-being. While some merely rest quietly, most of them sleep during nap time.

After nap time and snacks, activities similar to those of the morning are often engaged in. For example, crafts, dramatic play, or cooking a snack are activities that children enjoy. Sometimes there may be an hour of quality children's television, but more often the time is spent playing and learning, indoors or out, perhaps constructing something from wood or other materials. In a good program television watching is kept to a minimum.

The entire program of the center or day-care home should reflect the combined efforts of the staff working cooperatively. The specific types of activities are limited only by the skill and imagination of the people who will be caring for your children each day.

The close of the day is as important as the beginning. Each child should feel that the time was spent in a stimulating and satisfying way. Parents need to know about their child's progress and be made to feel welcome at the beginning and end of the day.

WHAT IS QUALITY CHILD CARE?

Every state has laws regulating family day-care homes and centers. They must be licensed, certified, or registered, according to each individual state's laws. Although there has been some discussion about establishing a model state licensing code, not much has been done to implement this as yet.

Every center must have a license. You should ask to see the center's license when you go to visit. These licenses are meant to insure that the center meets certain health and safety standards. Usually the licensing inspector visits the program before it begins operation and then returns for follow-up visits and for license renewal. If the facility has funding from the federal government, then federal interagency day-care requirements apply. The way to learn about day-care licensing requirements is to contact your state or county day-care office. See the Appendix for the agency in your state.

Child-care programs should be more than just custodial. The child-care center, as suggested by the proposed federal guidelines and state regulations, must offer a planned program of age-appropriate activities that provide for the mental, social, intellectual, and emotional development of the child. The daily programs must be described in writing. These planned activities must meet the developmental needs of the children. Examples of daily scheduled activities that children can count on are: conversation among children and care givers, opportunity for the child to play (including outdoor play when possible), time for rest, and participation in a variety of projects (cooking, looking at books, magazines, taking walks, playing games, and singing songs).

Another requirement for licensing is the provision of a variety of play materials. Older children must have opportunities for play and exercise with supervision, while infants should have space to crawl about, and sufficient staff to hold them, talk to them, and feed them.

The centers are also required to provide a trained and competent staff. The purpose of training for the staff is to acquaint them with patterns of child growth and development and to insure that they develop and sustain the skills necessary to satisfy the children's needs. They require previous orientation and training of all care givers and specialized training related to child care. Training should include handling behavior problems, ways of working with parents, nutrition and good eating, health and safety, design and use of space. All of these are seen as factors that relate to the child's well-being in the program.

The federal guidelines recommend that child-care centers provide nutritious meals and snacks, and that the parents be given written menus for the week. In the area of health, the center should have a medical history of each child and the child should receive a health assessment. The guidelines also recommend that the center plans to respond to illness and emergencies, and that they have these plans in writing. It is suggested that parents receive information on health services available in the community, and are guided in locating the right services. In addition, first-aid equipment should be on hand, lead-free paint should be used throughout the facility, and immunizations should be required for all children. There should be procedures for reporting suspected cases of child abuse and neglect.

Also the guidelines recommend that parents have adequate opportunities to observe and discuss the children's needs. Parents must be informed about the program and be able to exchange information with other parents. Parents can communicate through periodic meetings together, observation sessions, conferences, and parent advisory councils. Parents should have opportunities to evaluate the program, review budgeting, and learn parenting skills at parent education classes. All information should be provided in the primary language of the parents. The guidelines recommend that state agencies provide a checklist to aid parents in assessing the quality of children's day care, to establish procedures for raising any questions about the programs, and to have information-referral services to help other parents in locating day care.

The standards for day-care homes are also included in the federal guidelines. These standards should be considered the minimum for any program that you would consider for your child.

How the center or home establishes policy will affect you as a parent. You should pay close attention to the degree of responsibility, responsiveness, and caring shown by the staff and management. Observe the behavior of the children as they come to and from the program. Are they happy and satisfied? Do they look eager to be there? Watch how the staff interact with each other, talking about the children and about what is happening. Do they seem interested and involved?

Mealtime often gives a clue to the real quality of the program. It should be a sociable and relaxed time. Menus should be varied, nutritious, and interesting.

Observe the quality of the materials and equipment used by the children. The space should be organized so that the children are free to move around safe from accidents. There should be places to talk and to be private. A list of equipment and supplies for a typical program is in the Resources Appendix in the back of the book.

In relation to the staff, their attitude should be one of caring, it should be nonsexist and show a sensitivity to the children's problems. There should be opportunities for the children to express their feelings and for the staff to deal with behavior problems in a constructive way. Attitudes should be positive and energetic.

The children should enjoy being with each other and care about each other and one another's well-being. The care givers should talk in an easy, comfortable way with each other and should work well together.

Most parents know instinctively when they have found the right place. Not only will they have something to say about what goes on, they will be given the information they need and they will feel comfortable about the safety of their child. We interviewed many parents who said they knew immediately, by the way the staff spoke and reacted to them, whether it was a good program. Equipment and facilities aside, the staff is the key to making a program work.

Who Are the Child-Care Givers?

POINTS TO LOOK FOR

Everybody has some idea of what makes for a successful staff. The most important qualities of a successful child-care giver are listed here for you to review with a yes or no when you make your visits:

1. Are they able to talk easily with children?
2. Do they know about the special needs of each child?
3. Do they respond positively, sensitively, patiently?
4. Do they have a sense of humor?
5. Do they listen to the children and answer their questions?
6. Do they encourage each child to use his or her imagination and creative skills?
7. Are they competent in what they do?
8. Do they respect the individual differences of each child?
9. Do they create a warm and loving atmosphere?
10. Do they manage discipline without hurting the child?
11. Do they allow the children to work out their differences and solve problems without too much interference?
12. Is there a personal awareness of how their moods, voice tone, and behavior affect the children's behavior?
13. Do they respect each child and family and communicate easily with the parents?
14. Do they share parents' philosophies about children? And respect the parents' points of view?
15. Do they assist each child in developing good health habits?
16. Do they express love to the children?
17. Do they respond to your needs and keep appointments?
18. Do they take time to explain details?
19. Do they seem happy to have you visit and participate?

If you have a child that is an infant or below age three, the training and supervision will be better in a program that is specifically set up to care for infants. Here is a list of questions about the infant child-care giver:

Who Are the Child-Care Givers? | 39

Yes/No
1. Enjoys being with babies?
2. Has patience, warmth, and a nurturing attitude?
3. Knows that infants need to be talked to and cuddled?
4. Is aware of their nutritional needs?
5. Provides space where infants can play and crawl?
6. Promotes active cooperation between parents and staff?
7. Knows how to handle emergencies?
8. Is in good health and has plenty of energy?
9. Provides activities that are stimulating and appropriate to the baby's age?
10. Understands and cooperates with the parent's efforts to toilet train?

If your child is age three to six, these questions are important to consider when selecting a child-care giver:

Yes/No
1. Communicates with the child, talking, reading, and teaching new words?
2. Responds to each child in a warm and loving way?
3. Respects the individual differences of the child?
4. Has positive self-image?
5. Is energetic and imaginative in choosing activities?

If your child is between age six and twelve, these additional questions are important:

Yes/No
1. Respects the child's need for independence and dependency?
2. Is able to respond to the child's invidiual needs?
3. Respects the child's ideas and values?
4. Is willing to cooperate and sets clear limits of behavior?
5. Expresses a positive image for the child to respond to?

Of the many characteristics we seek in child-care givers the most important is that the care givers listen and respond to the child.

Children need adults to listen and respond to them. They need to know they matter, that they are important. They need guidance and help. Children like adults who are flexible and positive. Fairness is another important characteristic. Care givers should never ridicule or shame a child or use harsh methods of discipline. Regardless of family circumstances, all children need limits and to be treated with humor and common sense.

During your visit note how the care givers respond after the child accomplishes a task. See if they treat boys and girls differently. There should be no discrimination in their attitudes or behavior. Regardless of the child's ethnic background, they should respect the child's culture, language, and family values.

It is critically important that the people that work with children have no physical, emotional, or mental conditions that preclude them from working effectively, such as illness, hostility, or incompetence. They should have periodic X rays and TB tests, and be free of communicable diseases. They must have a working knowledge of first aid and emergency care. Records of each staff person's medical history should be on file in the office. They must be emotionally stable and be positive in their attitudes toward children.

The program should have a regular procedure for interviewing and screening potential employees. It is important to remember that credentials alone do not ensure quality care. Despite impressive credentials, some people may be unable to relate to small children or be inconsistent in discipline or have other deficits. Many care givers without formal training are naturally giving and loving with children.

More and more programs are learning the value of having male staff members. Children whose parents have divorced or who lack a father's presence in the home, as well as others, greatly benefit from the presence of male staff.

Meeting with parents is extremely valuable for the staff. Even the most experienced professionals can benefit from discussions with the parents, which enable them to cope more effectively with problems that crop up.

ADULT-TO-CHILD RATIOS

You will need to look at the number of children in the group in relation to the number of adults. For some time there has been a great controversy centered on this ratio. The following are the recommended ratios of adults to children for federally funded programs.

for day-care homes:
 3–4 adults to 4 children
 4–6 adults to 7 children
 6 or more adults to 10 or more children.

for child-care centers:
 1 adult to each of six children
 2–9 adults to 6 or more children

THE STAFF

Many different people work in child-care services. The director who determines the overall program has training in childhood education, plus any special training necessary to qualify this person for a particular program, such as Montessori training. The teachers will vary in skills, backgrounds, and ages. Their training is important, as is their attitude, their experience with children, and their personal philosophies.

The program may include volunteers, such as students and senior citizens. Students need to have an opportunity to learn about children and to experience them directly. High school students who volunteer in child care find that they learn important skills in parenting. Students often improve their grades in school as a result of working in a child-care situation.

Many older persons enjoy participating in child-care services. They have rich experience to offer the children. Being with the children helps alleviate loneliness and gives them a feeling of contributing to their community. Having senior citizens and children together works well for members of both groups.

Social workers may be employed by the center to help with any problems the children may have with each other and with the staff.

Psychologists can be on call for particular problems, and children can be referred to a child psychologist if the staff and parents feel this is desirable. Problems may arise from a traumatic or stressful event, such as a death or a divorce in the family.

Other members of the community, such as designers and architects, community planners, contractors, and researchers, may be part of the staff. Business and community leaders may be interested in child care and be willing to invest some of their time by serving on the program's board of directors.

TEEN-AGE MOTHERS

Child care also serves the larger community. For example, a program for pregnant teen-agers helps to keep teens in school while learning parenting. Ellen Galinsky in *The New Extended Family: Daycare That Works* describes individual programs for teen-age mothers. In the Durham School program in Philadelphia the child-care service includes a course in parenting: a combination of classes and on-the-spot observation and work. The pregnant teen-age girls' classroom connects with the center. Part of the day is spent in the center itself. Before her own baby is born each girl takes care of another baby in the center. A professional care giver is present to help her learn about child care. She learns not only by watching the care givers; she also assumes responsibility for some of the children for some time during the day. She is involved in diaper changing, feeding, cuddling, and infant stimulation. The director comments, "We aren't too concerned about the education; we can handle that if we can get the girl into the nursery and comfortable with being a parent. The rest will fall into place."

Child Care Corner in Minneapolis has a number of representatives of local senior citizens' organizations on its board of directors. The directors of child-care services have gone to senior citizens centers and conducted workshops. At Christmastime, they open a workshop in which senior citizens make toys for their grandchildren. In addition to these activities, senior citizens assist by reading, talking, or just being with children. They contribute enormously to the children's development in a variety of ways. Older citizens want to be involved and child care offers them a wonderful opportunity.

Whether one considers child care from the point of view of the baby, the toddler or older child, or the parents view, it is an enormously important community service. The involvement of all segments of the community ensures a higher level of service for everyone living and working there.

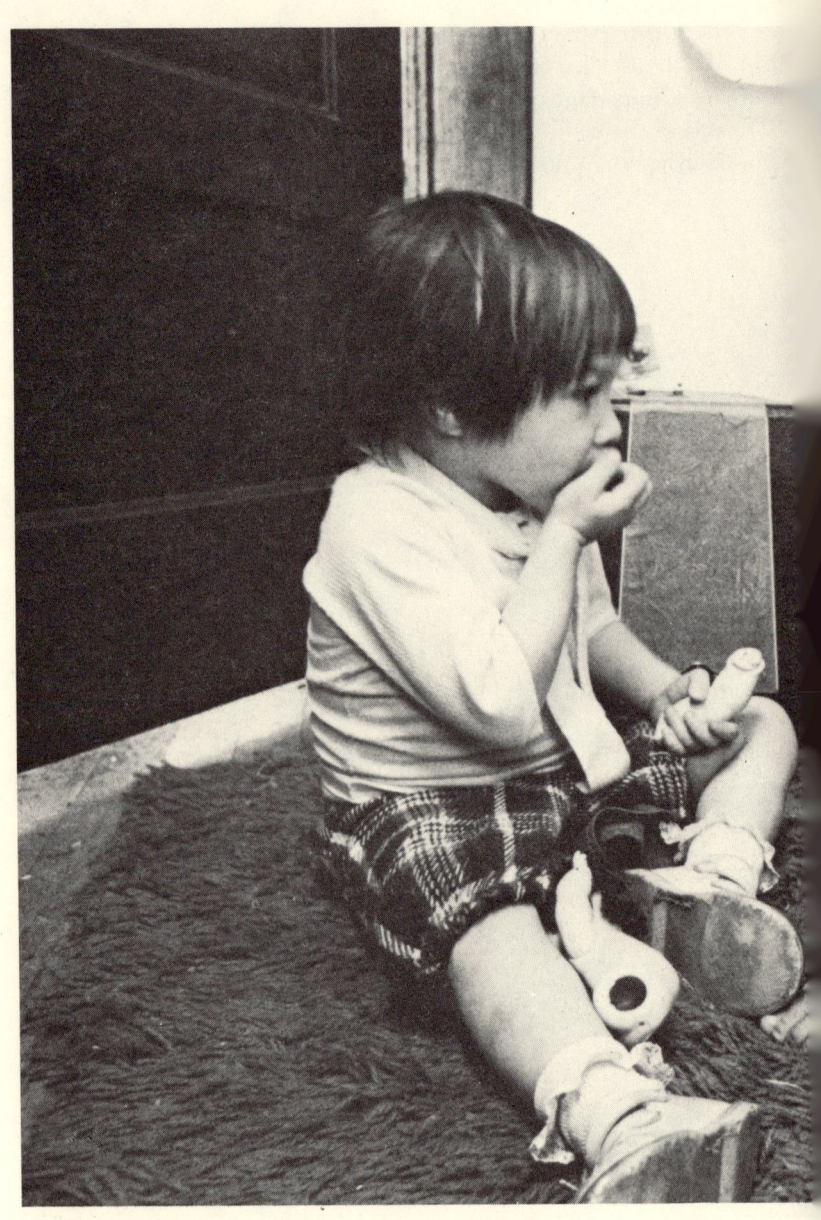

7 / Sitters

WHY HAVE A SITTER?

A sitter is someone who comes to your home or lives in your home. Sometimes a sitter is a relative or a friend who serves without pay. More often they are employees who receive a salary.

Why choose a baby-sitter or in-home care giver? If you have three or more children, you may find it is less expensive to have them cared for in your home, and it will save you the inconvenience of getting your children to and from child-care arrangements. If your child is under five, or has any special physical or emotional problems, then your child may feel more secure at home. If you work at night, then a sitter in the home is preferable, as the child cannot easily be taken out of the home at night, and outside care is hard to find after 6:00 P.M.

The drawbacks to having an in-home sitter are:

1. the lack of supervision,
2. the lack of stimulation of being with other children, and
3. the cost and risks involved in depending on one person who may or may not show up on any one day.

INTERVIEWING A SITTER

To find a sitter, place an ad in your local newspaper, or put up a notice at the post office, local laundromat, community center, or any location where people may come who you feel would be competent to care for your child. If you advertise you may receive many calls. Talk to each person for five to ten minutes. This should be a quiet, uninterrupted time, so the caller and you can relax and talk easily. If either of you is hurried, ask the person to call back and set a time for the return call.

During the call you should:

1. Explain your situation briefly.
2. Find out about the person's background and experience.
3. Write down the names and phone numbers of references, names of previous employers, length of time worked and duties.
4. Get a sense of what this person is like, whether you feel good about him or her and what he or she has to offer.

If you think the person is a good possibility, ask the following questions:

1. Do you want a regular situation now?
2. For how long would you be interested in working?
3. How do you think children should be disciplined? (Allow them time to explain how they would handle your child.)
4. What are your thoughts about preparing food or feeding children? About toilet habits?
5. Do you have any health problems that will affect your work?
6. Do you drive?
7. Do you drink? Smoke?
8. Have you had a medical check-up and X rays recently?
9. Do you know different activities to do with children? (Ask them to describe some of the activities they like to do with children.)
10. How do you feel about children watching television?

When you are interviewing a teen-ager or college student for an after-school job, ask if they have had experience caring for younger brothers and sisters and about other experiences with children.

After you have reviewed the important points over the phone and are satisfied, then arrange for your prospective sitter to come to your house. Be sure you give them good directions to locate the place you live. Show your prospective sitter around the house and describe the things you want him or her to do. Introduce the person to your child or children and note their reactions. It is important that they relate well to each other.

FOLLOW-UP

For the person you hire you should spell out exactly the terms of employment; this will include:

1. the hours of work
2. salary
3. Social Security and income tax deductions
4. sick leave
5. vacations

6. insurance
7. when salary will be paid and whether in cash or check
8. additional duties expected, such as housekeeping, shopping or meal preparation
9. rules regarding drinking, smoking, television watching, visitors, and telephone use.

The prospective sitter should make notes of what is said. Be sure to explain to the sitter what your child is like, how your home operates, what he or she can expect in terms of snacks and food. If you do not want the sitter to have people over when you are away or not to use your telephone, be sure to tell him so right away. Put in writing anything that is necessary for emergencies, including a medical release form. Put the form and other written instructions and phone numbers in a permanent place next to the telephone. The instructions should include numbers for where you can be reached and for a close relative or friend the sitter can get in touch with during the day if you are not easily available. Also list numbers for the doctor, fire department, police, ambulance; list the child's routines, special toys and equipment, any special problems with the house, off-limit areas, your child's allergies, and so forth.

Check the house to see if there are any potential hazards the sitter should know about. Make sure the sitter knows how to apply first aid and where the first-aid kit is. You may want to put together a baby-sitter's kit, containing pencils and crayons, paper, yarn, envelopes, toys, tissues, flashlight, adhesive bandages, books, and magazines. Some excellent additional handbooks and guides to baby-sitting are included in Further Reading, which follows the Resources Appendix.

See if the person seems flexible, has a warm and affectionate nature, and responds and talks easily to the child. If he or she moves in too quickly on the child, or gushes, or is too sweet, the child may be turned off. It is better if the child comes to him or her. If at all possible, check references and talk to one or two of the poeple he or she has worked for. The relationship between the sitter and the parent should be honest and open. You want the sitter to feel free to talk to you about the child's behavior while you are gone and to give you any additional information you need to know. Also make time to get to know the sitter on a personal basis—find out what he or she likes to do, about their family, and about their life. This person can be a real friend to you beyond the job itself. Your mutual relationship is important for the child's security and well-being.

8 / Homes

GATHERING INFORMATION ON THE TELEPHONE

Once you have put together a list of potential day-care homes, you will want to get as much information as possible over the phone. If the person you call is too busy to answer your questions, arrange to call back at a more convenient time.

Have paper and pencil ready. Write down:

1. The name of the day-care home
2. The address
3. The telephone number

Then ask and put down the answers to the following questions:

1. What is the experience and training of the care givers?
2. How long has the home been available for child care?
3. How many children are being cared for?
4. Is the home licensed?
5. Is care provided if the child becomes ill?
6. What provisions are made for emergencies?
7. What information is kept on each child?
8. Are parents expected to participate in the program?
9. Can you have the names of the parents who use the home?
10. Can you visit the home? If yes, arrange a time to do so.

WHAT TO LOOK FOR WHEN YOU VISIT

Note how long it takes you to get to the home and the distance traveled. Be prepared to give the care provider your work schedule, phone numbers at work, and other pertinent information. Observe the home's setting and how it relates to your views on child care.

You will want to pay particular attention to the personal characteristics of the care giver. You are looking for someone who has a positive awareness of children, is warm and affectionate, is consistent about setting limits, and knows how to respond to each child individually. Ask yourself the following:

1. Does this person make you feel welcome?
2. How does she relate to the children?

3. Is she enthusiastic and positive?
4. Does she use positive methods of discipline?
5. Does she listen to the children?
6. Is she in good health?
7. Does it seem she would respond well in an emergency?
8. Does she have an understanding of child growth and development?
9. Does she respect the children?
10. Does she have an attractive personality?

Take a careful look at the physical environment. There should be plenty of space for free movement and activities. The more attractive and comfortable the place is, the more positively the children will respond.

Indoors, ask yourself the following:

1. Is there enough space for children to play?
2. Is there a balance between active and quiet areas? (Children need places where they can be by themselves, to be quiet, study, or rest.)

For the outdoors:

1. Is there enough space for children to play that is away from traffic and other dangers?
2. Is there a park nearby for more active play?

The overall quality of the home will depend on the person in charge and the staff. There should be enough adults to give the children the individual attention they need.

If the day-care home is state or federally funded, it must meet state or federal requirements for day-care homes. The conditions for qualifying for funding are:

1. the home provides snacks and meals,
2. there is available training for staff,
3. utilization of health and social services
4. medical records should be kept for each child.

CHOOSING CHILD CARE | 54

It is required that a working relationship be developed with a health-care professional who provides appropriate care for sick children. Emergency numbers must be by the telephone and first-aid materials handy, facilities must be painted with lead-free base paint, and the children must be immunized, as well as other precautions such as infant restraints, sufficient numbers of safe toys, and playground equipment and materials.

Here is a list of specific things you want to look for:

1. A safe bathroom
2. A safe appliance area
3. Lead-free paint (ask, just in case)
4. Play areas clear of clutter
5. Private rest areas where sick children can be quiet
6. Safe childproof electrical sockets
7. Skid-proof rugs
8. A personal drinking glass or paper cups
9. The practice of consistent safety measures
10. A clean and comfortable environment
11. A nutritious and balanced menu
12. Snacks provided
13. Limits on or no "junk" food
14. Food not withheld as punishment
15. Children participate in play as they would at home
16. Children are given choices of activities
17. Ample and varied materials provided for educational activities
18. An ample number of appropriate toys and play equipment provided
19. Children expected to help put things away
20. Television watching kept to a minimum and carefully selected
21. Nap time rules enforced
22. Balanced rest and play activities
23. A variety of interesting books available
24. The care giver reads aloud to the children
25. Arrangements can be made for care during sick days
26. Care is provided on vacations and holidays

For further items worthy of attention, refer to the checklists in chapter 10. Many of the criteria by which we evaluate child-care centers apply equally well to day-care homes.

FOLLOW-UP

The family day-care home has the responsibility to provide the toys, facilities, and supervision necessary for programs that are safe, stimulating, and interesting for a child. Your responsibility is to be sure to deliver and pick up your child on time. Discuss this with the care giver but usually you may bring along any items your child may need, such as special food, favorite toys, diapers, a change of clothing, and a toothbrush. Make sure you give the care giver any necessary special instructions. Talk with the care giver about holidays, emergencies, and vacations. If the home is providing before- and after-school care, make sure you report the hours your child is in school and under what special circumstances the child can have friends over after school (with agreement). Also reach agreements on how and when payment is to be made, whether in cash or check, and if there are any fees or charges for time missed, and any other additional responsibilities. Agree on terms for ending the arrangement. After you have gone over the arrangements and the specific agreements, put them on paper, so that they can be referred to at a later time by both of you to avoid misunderstandings and problems later on.

Family day-care homes can give children security and stability, while providing for each child's individual differences. Many family day-care homes are being linked, through networks and other organizational systems, with other programs that provide services such as counseling, housecleaning, staff-training workshops, and parenting workshops.

Family day-care homes provide care at moderate cost. They can be convenient to your work or your home. As a nurturing environment for your child while you are at work, they can be an excellent child-care arrangement.

CHECKLIST

GATHERING FACTS ON THE DAY-CARE HOME

1. Name _____ Phone _____

   Address _____

   Experience _____

2. Length of time home has been operating _____

3. Transportation easy? Yes _____ No _____

4. Is the home licensed? Yes _____ No _____ Did you see the license? Yes _____ No _____

5. Can the provider care for a child who becomes ill or has an accident? Yes _____ No _____ Is a first-aid kit available? Yes _____ No _____ Is emergency care available? Yes _____ No _____ Is there an "emergency form" available giving your permission for care, just in case? Yes _____ No _____

6. Does the home keep information/records on the child and his or her development? Yes _____ No _____

7. Are parents expected to be part of the program? Yes _____ No _____

8. Can you have the names of other parents who use the home? Yes _____ No _____

Names and phone numbers of other parents _____

_____

_____

9. Can you visit? Yes _____ No _____

Date of visit _____

Overall impression: Excellent _____ Good _____ Fair _____ Poor _____

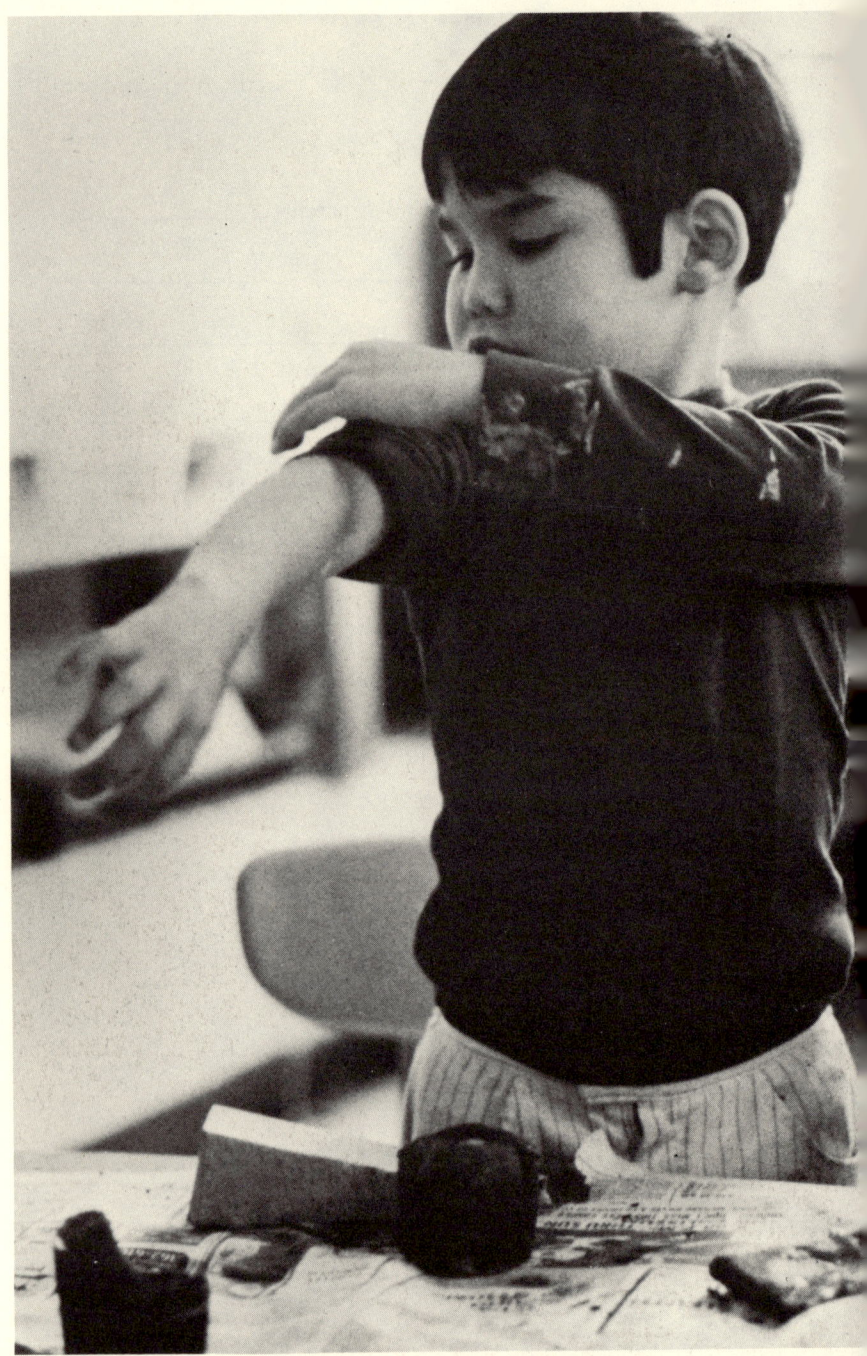

9 / Centers

CHOOSING CHILD CARE | 60

At a center children are cared for in a group. Centers can have few or many children. Some care for as many as 150 children. Some centers take care of children before they go to school, some care for children after school, some do both. Some care for preschool children only, for a half day or a full day. Child-care centers may be privately run or sponsored by the government, churches, community organizations, employers, unions, or other groups. The programs are usually run by teachers, who have specialized training in early childhood education.

Your community may have a private or franchised center that is part of a for-profit company in the business of child care. Some of the franchised centers are: Living and Learning, Mary Moppets, Kinder-care, Amerikid, Mini-skools, and Les Petits Academies. Many of these programs do meet children's needs and have good facilities. The teachers generally are trained by the company. Mini-skools, located at Newport Beach, California, has eighty day-care centers in the United States and Canada. They enroll children up to six years of age. They emphasize a physical environment where the children are safe and are given good care during the day. But services of franchised centers vary from place to place. Check to see what is included at your local for-profit center; not all private programs are consistently good. You have to weigh each program separately.

Some employers provide their employees with child care at the place of employment or at a nearby privately operated program. The employees' children are guaranteed a place at these child-care centers.

Frequently, colleges and universities will have child-care centers, sometimes connected with the student unions or the Education Department, operated by the students or faculty. The one problem with these programs is that they are closed during the school holidays and the summer. This may be inconvenient if you are working besides attending the school.

Other programs are subsidized by state and federal dollars. They are run by a local government agency and serve low- and middle-income families. Usually the fees are on a sliding scale. Sometimes these programs are underfunded, understaffed, and overenrolled. You want to be sure this is not the case with the program you choose for your child.

Another kind of program is the drop-in center. Here the charge is by the hour. They may be operated in connection with a shopping center or college, and they are convenient for short-term situations.

There are centers that offer special services to handicapped children and a highly trained staff is available to meet complex needs. Sometimes child-care centers are associated with hospitals and schools. Child care is becoming more readily accepted, understood, and supported in the community at large.

During your visit you should observe the activities and the way the children are treated and the general atmosphere of the place. You should be able to talk with the director of each center and get answers to some of your questions before you visit. You will want your child to visit for a while before you make a final decision.

Your observation of the program is extremely important. You want to compare the number of children to the number of adults active in their care. This is called the child/staff ratio. The number of adults per child is an important indication of the quality of the program. For example, one care giver is recommended for every four to five children under the age of three, while there should be one care giver for every seven to nine children between the ages of three and five.

In addition, you should notice the number of children in small groups within the larger group. It is recommended that there be no more than twenty children in a group of three- to five-year-olds, and less than twelve to a group if they are under three.

Notice the amount of attention children get from each adult. See how they are cared for and, when problems come up, how they are handled. Notice the interaction between children. See the quality of the activities, the variety, their appropriateness for the age level of the children. Are activities interesting to the children? Are they easy to understand and yet challenging? Do the children seem happy, at ease, involved? Does the staff seem to be patient and enjoy being with the children?

You will need to provide the center with the following information:

1. Your name
2. Your address

3. Your phone number (at home)
4. Your child's name
5. The birthdate, height, and weight of your child
6. Phone numbers where the parents are during the day
7. Work schedule
8. Emergency numbers of a friend or relative, and doctor and/or dentist
9. Medical information, dates of immunizations, any allergies, last physical examination
10. Special needs or problems, medications
11. Information on development (ages your child walked and talked)
12. Health habits, eating, sleeping, etc.
13. Information on brothers and sisters, ages and special considerations
14. Income and related financial information if you are applying for aid
15. Transportation needs

Most centers require the child to have a recent physical examination and have all necessary immunizations.

If the program you are considering requires you to sign a contract these items will be in the agreement:

1. Fees you will pay
2. Due dates of payments
3. Days your child will come to the center
4. Hours your child will be there
5. How you will transport the child to and from center

The contract should also cover anything else that is important. Before you sign the document, ask any questions that occur to you. Bring a copy of the contract home to show your partner and to keep in your files.

Keep the contract handy. It may specify what items the director expects parents to bring for the children, such as changes of clothing, special toys, and educational materials.

NOTE ON INFANT CARE

Infant care outside the home has been a controversial subject for some time. If you have a sitter in your home, you may have no more guarantee of quality care than you would if your child was in a family day-care home, a sitter's home, or a center specially designed for the care of infants. However, the quality of the supervision, training, and other benefits obviously will be greater in those places designed and licensed specifically to care for infants.

What to look for:
1. A small number of infants with each adult
2. Care givers who interact warmly and affectionately
3. A place well designed for the infants to play, move, and crawl about in safety
4. Active cooperation between parents and staff so they both know and understand each other and the individual needs of the infant

The characteristics you will want to look for in the care giver are: patience, warmth, and a nurturing attitude toward infants. The care giver should be a person who likes infants and recognizes their need to be talked to, cuddled, and allowed to crawl about. The care giver should be in good health and have the energy and interest to provide the balanced care so vital to a young baby. The program should offer sufficient individual attention, feeding, diapering, time for sleeping, a lot of affection and stimulation, and provisions for emergency care. The staff should encourage verbal and motor development on a continuous and consistent basis.

Children's needs begin at birth and change and develop throughout their early years. The more the care giver knows and understands these needs, the greater the likelihood that the program will promote your infant's growth and well-being.

AFTER-SCHOOL CARE

When children reach kindergarten or first grade and through most of their elementary school years, their capacity for independence steadily increases. However, they still require supervision and attention. Many children, because of the scarcity of sufficient after-school arrangements, are "latch-key" children and return to their homes with no one there to greet and care for them. They are often lonely and have only a TV for company.

Fortunately, many improvements are now taking place. More and more schools are staying open after 3:00 P.M. to provide interesting after-school recreation and arts and crafts. Many family day-care homes also provide after-school care. Children at this age want to have a place to go, friends to play with, and engaging activities to occupy them. It is also a comfort to them to have an adult to turn to.

At this age, children like dramatics, music, dance, crafts, art projects, games of all kinds, and sports. They like to be able to choose from a number of possible activities. Being part of a supervised group after school fills two needs, the need for security and the need for amusement while the parents are away.

THE DISABLED CHILD

More schools, centers, and homes are offering opportunities for children with various degrees of disability to be enrolled in programs with normal children. Keeping the special needs of your child in mind, you may be able to use one of the child-care alternatives already suggested.

The program should provide, in addition to very well-qualified and sensitive teachers, the on-call resources of a nurse, speech therapist, physical therapist, and other specialists as required. The physical space should be easy for the child to move around in, with a well-defined program where each child can find interesting and enjoyable activities to engage in according to ability. The relationship between you and the care giver will be very important, as both of you will be committed to providing important learning and social experiences for your child.

WHAT TO LOOK FOR

Environment. Notice whether the surroundings are safe and whether the children are free to move around. There should be a balance between the indoor and outdoor spaces and a place for children to be private. The overall environment should be appropriate for their age, stimulating to them and helpful for learning.

Nutrition. The menus should be nutritionally well-balanced and varied. Notice whether there are a variety of good snacks available, such as peanuts, crackers, raisins, carrots, celery, juice, and so forth. You will also want to notice the amount of sugar that is offered. It is highly recommended that the amount of sugar given a child be limited. In a good program the children enjoy mealtime and the meals are served in comfortable, relaxed family style. Children need to be encouraged to feed themselves and to have interesting talk at mealtime. The portions should be the right size for them, and they should be encouraged to try new foods. The center can expand their tastes beyond what you can do at home because children respond to other children's interests.

Toilet training. It is preferable that the child be toilet trained before she or he enters the program. If it is a center that cares for infants, see if there are special places for diapering. The older child should have easy access to a bathroom whenever he needs one.

Health. Ask the director about what type of services are available, and whether there is a pediatrician or doctor on call. Availability of dental services is also important, and the children should have a place to brush their teeth.

Rest. Children need a regular rest time and a place where they can sleep and be quiet on a cot or a pad.

Toys. Some programs allow the child to bring a favorite toy. Observe what is available and, if you wish, ask the director about bringing a toy from home.

Illness. Usually, children are not allowed to come to the center if they have a communicable disease. However, if the child becomes ill during the day, there should be a quiet space where the child can be taken care of. If the center agrees to care for a child who is ill, then be sure to give instructions to the director on care and dispensation of medications during the day.

Education. Make sure that all your questions about the educational services of the program are answered. Any questions your child may have should be answered also. How the staff responds is an important indication of the overall quality of the program. Children should be able to make decisions and discuss their needs with the staff and the director. You will want to notice whether the children have opportunities to talk among themselves, to share and discuss ideas, and whether they feel free to express themselves. You will want to know what kind of schedule the educational program follows each day. You can follow up at home by reading, talking, and practicing skills with your child.

Acknowledgment and attention. The way in which the children are greeted on arriving is important. You will want to know how and by whom this is done each day. It is important to say hello and goodbye to children as they come and go each day. You will want to notice whether the small groups of children are happy, active, and involved. If the atmosphere in the program is informal and the children seem to be treated with consideration and respect, you will have a good indication that the program is of good quality.

Atmosphere. You will know you are in a good program if children feel free and comfortable with each other and the adults. If children appear to have their problems resolved with a minimum of physical aggressiveness, if children seem to work and play well together, and if the attitude appears to be one of cooperation and enjoyment, you can feel confident about the program. Discipline should be fair and not abusive. Special occasions, such as birthdays, should be observed.

Activities. Look for a balance between work and play. Time should be allowed for cleaning up and for toys to be put away. You want to be sure the children have a variety of interesting activities to engage in, that there is freedom to talk, move, and interact with each other, that there is time for snacks, for play outdoors, and trips to places in the neighboring area. Notice the kinds and number of toys, equipment, and furniture, how the toys are stored, whether they are sturdy and of good quality, and whether they can be reached easily.

If there is outdoor play, the center should have climbing materials, and equipment that can take hard wear, sand, and dirt. For adequate movement, approximately seventy-five square feet per child is usually recommended. Indoors thirty-five square feet is considered adequate. The physical space inside should be clear of obstructions; basic standards of cleanliness and safety should be met; fabrics should be fire-resistant; first-aid equipment accessible. There should be no poisonous substances nearby, and the entire facility should be painted with lead-free paint (ask about the safety features). Check to see that the temperature is comfortable, and that there is adequate light and ventilation. In the checklist at the end of chapter 10 we have included a list of recommended equipment, toys, and related items.

CHECKLIST

GATHERING FACTS ON A CHILD-CARE CENTER

1. Name of director _____ Phone _____

    Name and address of center _____

2. Name of the person who will provide the care _____

    Experience of the care giver _____

3. Transportation easy? Yes _____ No _____

4. Does the center have a license? Yes _____ No _____ Did you see the license? Yes _____ No _____

5. Length of time center has been operating _____

6. Is there a first-aid kit? Yes _____ No _____ Is emergency care available when the child becomes ill? Yes _____ No _____

7. Does the center keep information/records on the children and his or her development? Yes_____ No_____

8. Are parents expected to be part of the center? Yes_____ No_____

9. Will the director provide you with the names of other parents who use the center? Yes_____ No_____

Names and phone numbers of parents _____

_____

_____

10. Can you visit? Yes_____ No_____

Date of visit _____

Overall impression: Excellent_____ Good_____ Fair_____ Poor_____

10 / Looking at the Checklist

The checklist serves as a clear and concise guide of what to look for when you visit. Each place will be different, although you may find certain similarities.

You will want to visit as many places as you can. Use the checklist each time. Record your answers for each place on a separate piece of paper. In this way you can record your impressions on each place and review them later.

Look at the whole place, inside and out. Is the center inviting and a nice place to be? Words like *homey* and *comfortable* or *cold* and *cluttered* might occur to you. Is the place well arranged and attractive, or is it crowded and impersonal? You will get a sense of these things as you move around and observe.

You may feel uncomfortable about taking the checklist into the place you are visiting. If so, become thoroughly familiar with what the checklist covers and remember the questions. Then you can leave the checklist in your purse and fill it out right after you complete each visit.

Child-care providers should welcome the parent's concern and interest. An informed parent is an asset to any child-care situation. If the care-giver appears to feel uncomfortable by being judged in this way, try to be sensitive to this feeling while you gather your information as unobtrusively as possible. You should take as much time as you need for this process. Two hours is a good amount of time to learn about a child-care center—to talk with the director, with the teacher, and see the children move through several different activities. If you are not certain after reviewing the checklist and your feelings about the center, pay another visit or talk with other parents about their feelings. Try to attend a parent-teacher meeting. Good communication between the staff and parents is one of the important ways to make the child-care situation successful for everyone.

The physical facility checklist. The physical space in which a child spends time is very important. Environment is critical to growth and development. The space allocated should be at least thirty-five square feet for every child enrolled. While you will want to check out safety and creative use of the play areas and equipment, keep in mind that an older place lacking the latest or fanciest equipment often has many other features that make it more than adequate.

Looking at the Checklist | 71

The emotional climate checklist. What happens emotionally to the children in the environment is most critical. A place that needs paint can still be a place of love and attention. Beyond the basic care they need, children are affected by the way staff interact with them and the other children. Among other important concerns, you, as a parent, need to know how discipline is handled and how comfortable the children are with each other.

The learning climate checklist. An important part of any child-care program is the number and quality of learning opportunities offered. Trips and extra activities add richness to the overall program. Child care can prepare your child for the lifelong enjoyment of learning and education, both in formal schooling and outside of school.

Parents should be able to follow their child's learning progress in the center or home. The staff should keep the parents informed about the child's progress. The parents also learn from their child's experiences, from the teachers, and from each other.

The social climate checklist. A vital part of any program is the opportunity the center or home provides for the children to get to know each other and contribute something special to each other. When the staff relate to the children in a warm and supportive way, children respond happily. They learn easily and play with each other contentedly. Children who haven't had the attention and support demanded by the more assertive children are shy.

Observing. Don't judge by surface appearances. Toys, books, and fancy materials can be deceptive. Try to look beyond the children's cute appearances or smiles and actually see what they are expressing, feeling, and doing. Try to imagine how it would feel to be them and how your child would relate to these adults and children. In some situations the staff may restrain the children from expressing themselves fully or comfortably.

Using the checklist. Arrange for your visit over the phone with the director or care giver. This is the person who generally greets you when you arrive at the center or home.

As you walk around the place, your discussion should cover the points mentioned on each list.

During your visit or immediately afterward fill in the response that fits best for each question.

THE PHYSICAL FACILITY CHECKLIST

1. Does the space seem safe? (Lights and electric sockets covered or out-of-reach or safety type?)

    Yes_____ No_____

2. Is there enough space, well planned, without crowding?

    Yes_____ No_____

3. Is the equipment inside and out varied, sturdy, safe, and easy for a child to use?

    Yes_____ No_____

4. Is the place attractive and comfortable? (Are there plants, pets, and special activity areas?)

    Yes_____ No_____

5. Can the children get inside and outside safely and without difficulty?

    Yes_____ No_____

6. Are the materials ample, in good condition, and easily available? (Can children reach a variety of books, toys, art supplies, etc.?)

    Yes_____ No_____

7. Are the bathroom facilities clean and easy for a child to use? (Easy-to-reach faucets, toilets, toothbrushes and toothpaste, paper-towels, etc.?)

    Yes_____ No_____

8. Are the meals nutritious and well balanced, and is the food prepared and served attractively?

    Yes_____ No_____

Looking at the Checklist | 73

9. Do the children have a comfortable and quiet place for naps?

　　　　　　　　　　　　　　　　Yes_____ No_____

10. Does the place have provisions for an ill child? A first-aid kit? Staff who can assist in emergencies?

　　　　　　　　　　　　　　　　Yes_____ No_____

FINAL TALLY OF OBSERVATIONS ON PHYSICAL SPACE

　　　　　　　　　　Total number of YES answers_____

　　　　　　　　　　Total number of NO answers _____

Other words I would use to describe the place _____

_____

How would my child feel about this place? _____

_____

How do I feel about this place? _____

_____

THE EMOTIONAL CLIMATE CHECKLIST

1. Do the children show they really like and trust the adults?
　　　　　　　　　　　　　　　　Yes_____ No_____

2. Do the children appear happy, comfortable, and relaxed?
　　　　　　　　　　　　　　　　Yes_____ No_____

3. Does the staff communicate easily with each child?
　　　　　　　　　　　　　　　　Yes_____ No_____

4. Does the discipline reflect my philosophy?
　　　　　　　　　　　　　　　　Yes_____ No_____

5. Are the children allowed to pursue their own interests according to their abilities?

Yes_____ No_____

6. Are the children's emotional needs given first priority?

Yes_____ No_____

7. Would my child receive the attention he (or she) needs and be treated fairly here?

Yes_____ No_____

8. Are problems handled without upset?

Yes_____ No_____

9. Does the director or teacher answer my questions openly?

Yes_____ No_____

10. Do I feel comfortable with the staff and the place?

Yes_____ No_____

FINAL TALLY OF OBSERVATIONS ON EMOTIONAL CLIMATE

Total number of YES answers_____

Total number of NO answers _____

Words I would use to describe the emotional climate _____

_____

How would my child feel about this place?_____

_____

How do I feel about this place?_____

_____

THE LEARNING CLIMATE CHECKLIST

1. Is the place arranged for easy learning and growing?

    Yes_____ No_____

2. Does the program seem well planned?

    Yes_____ No_____

3. Does the program provide many different opportunities for the individual child?

    Yes_____ No_____

4. Can children move around and find materials easily?

    Yes_____ No_____

5. Are the learning opportunities suitable for the different age groups?

    Yes_____ No_____

6. Are the children's questions answered easily?

    Yes_____ No_____

7. Do the children enjoy the available activities?

    Yes_____ No_____

8. Do the children receive enough individual attention and assistance?

    Yes_____ No_____

9. Are special events and trips arranged frequently?

    Yes_____ No_____

10. Is the children's work, such as drawings and craft projects, displayed and discussed with the parents and available for the parents to take home?

    Yes_____ No_____

CHOOSING CHILD CARE | 76

FINAL TALLY OF OBSERVATIONS ON LEARNING CLIMATE

Total number of YES answers _____

Total number of NO answers _____

What is taught and how is it taught? _____

_____

Words I would use to describe the educational opportunities ___

_____

How do I feel about the learning opportunities here? _____

_____

THE SOCIAL CLIMATE CHECKLIST

1. Do I like how the children behave and relate to each other?
   Yes_____ No_____

2. Are conflicts handled with sensitivity?
   Yes_____ No_____

3. Would my child fit in with the group?
   Yes_____ No_____

4. Would my child make friends here?
   Yes_____ No_____

5. Are the language and culture of each child respected?
   Yes_____ No_____

6. Do the children respond easily and happily to each other?
   Yes_____ No_____

7. Do the children have many conflicts?
   Yes_____ No_____

8. Does the staff encourage children to express themselves and participate?

Yes_____ No_____

9. Are the children learning nonsexist social roles?

Yes_____ No_____

10. Are parents made to feel welcome and encouraged to know each other?

Yes_____ No_____

FINAL TALLY OF OBSERVATIONS ON SOCIAL CLIMATE

Total number of YES answers_____

Total number of NO answers _____

Words I would use to describe the social climate (advantages and disadvantages) _____

_____

How would I feel about being a parent in this place?_____

_____

How would my child feel in this place?_____

_____

RATING THE MOST IMPORTANT CHECKS

1. The place can be reached easily.

Yes_____ No_____

2. The place is safe, comfortable, and attractive.

Yes_____ No_____

3. The place has plenty of good and varied toys and equipment for fun and learning.

Yes_____ No_____

4. Children and staff interact happily and communicate easily.

Yes_____ No_____

5. The place offers nutritious, tasty meals and snacks.

Yes_____ No_____

6. Each child is respected as an individual.

Yes_____ No_____

7. Each child has the opportunity and space for a wide range of activities, either for playing with other children or for playing quietly by himself or herself.

Yes_____ No_____

8. My needs for the care giver to be dependable and value me as a parent are considered.

Yes_____ No_____

9. I can afford the fees at this place.

Yes_____ No_____

10. The place is suitable for my child and my situation.

Yes_____ No_____

RATING

Total number of items = 50

Total number of YES answers_____

Total number of NO answers _____

Total number of YES answers
- 40–50 Excellent program. Seriously consider it.
- 30–40 Good program. Think some more.

20–30 Fair program. Don't use it if you can avoid it.
Fewer than 20 Definitely continue your search.

A final comment on the checklist. If in each area—physical, emotional, learning, and social—you have more YES than NO answers, you have found a place that will probably care for your child well. If not, don't be discouraged. Continue your search until you find the most appropriate place for your child and one that will meet your standards for quality.

11 / Comparing and Choosing

By now you have visited a number of centers and homes and interviewed several sitters. Before you make your final selection, let's review your experience and reflect about what you are going to do next.

Take some time, sit down, and really think about all the things you've seen and heard. Separate the real possibilities from all the options. If you are still confused or uncertain about what you really want and need for your child and yourself, it's understandable. You will seldom find a perfect arrangement even when the place looks perfect on the surface.

By this time, you will, however, be pretty certain about what type of care will suit your child best—home, center, sitter, or alternative. You will probably choose the type of arrangement that most appeals to you and what you can afford. The discussion on planning your budget will assist you in reaching this decision.

In going through the checklists, match up the goals and needs of you and your child (as you defined them earlier) with what each situation has to offer. You might want to do this with a friend or adviser so you can be sure to consider all your options.

Which place feels best to you? Was it the way the place looked? Were the things provided for the children outstanding?

Did you like the way the staff knew each child and talked to each one?

Did the children seem to be happy, playful, and content?

How would your child fit in?

Is there anything further you want to know about the program?

If you have any doubts or want more information, contact a few of the parents to talk over your concerns and get answers to your questions.

Is the place convenient and accessible by car or public transportation?

Is it near your workplace?

Will your child receive good emergency care if an accident occurs or an illness arises?

Will the hours of the place coincide with your work schedule?

Will parent meetings and other commitments fit your time schedule?

Are these meetings arranged at convenient times with consideration for parents and children?

If you cannot attend evening meetings, are there other ways you can be involved in the program?

Are the other parents you have spoken with happy with the place, the staff, and the way their own children are making progress? If not, find out why.

Will you be allowed to be with your child the first days, until you and your child feel comfortable with the arrangement and adjust?

Can you visit when you want to?

If the answer to all of these questions is positive, and the fee fits your budget, this could be your best choice. If you have additional questions and are not certain, continue looking. This careful selection will pay off over time and is why the search often takes several weeks.

You might want to develop a secondary plan for child care for the future and put your name on the waiting list of your first choice. Maybe you can find room there later or a better arrangement in just six months or a year. What's your second choice if this situation doesn't work out? Often, as time goes on, you become more familiar with child-care opportunities in your local area, and selecting child care becomes easier. Contact the "Switchboard" or referral service regularly.

PLANNING A WORKABLE BUDGET

Shopping for child care is no simple matter, because you are dealing not just with simple fixed fees, but with an array of different and sometimes complicated eligibility requirements. As we stated elsewhere, the most expensive programs are not necessarily the best, and indeed, some of the best programs are the cheapest, if not free. It all depends on where the funds for the program come from—whether from the federal, state, or local government, from the school system or the welfare department, from private foundations, religious groups, private industry, or entirely from contributions by parents.

Many good programs accept only the children of welfare or poverty-level families. In these cases, having a job may disqualify you from the program. Other programs have fee scales based on income that may result in your paying a higher percentage of your income for child care as your income increases, leaving you with less money after a raise than before.

You must establish your personal priorities clearly. Bear in mind the effects your taking employment will have. Think about costs related to your taking a job. If you receive food stamps and/or public assistance, consider the effect working will have on your eligibility for these benefits.

We suggest that, before you commit yourself to work and child care, you consider alternative arrangements. Usually there is more than one combination of things you can do to meet your family and financial responsibilities and pursue your study or job and personal goals at the same time. It is a good idea to try to imagine yourself in each of these possibilities. For example, you could put your child on a waiting list for a center and find a part-time sitter so you can enroll in a training program. You could participate in a parent co-op and work part-time. You could use the skills you have to take a job that might not be entirely satisfying, but one that would pay enough for you to afford the child care while you support yourself and your family until you can locate the kind of job you want.

Give serious consideration to how you will make ends meet while providing for yourself and your children emotionally at the same time. List your alternatives on a piece of paper along with your goals and what you hope to accomplish and then think about it for a few days. It is important that you consider exactly what your expenses will be so you will be prepared for them.

Let's start by thinking through the expenses involved. Use this budget as a guide to list your alternatives.

BUDGET

	PLAN A	PLAN B	PLAN C
EXPECTED INCOME	JOB A	JOB B	JOB C
Annual	_____	_____	_____
Monthly Gross	_____	_____	_____
Take-Home (Net)	_____	_____	_____

EXPECTED MONTHLY EXPENSES

Rent	_____	_____	_____
Food	_____	_____	_____
Utilities	_____	_____	_____
Medical	_____	_____	_____
Other fixed payments	_____	_____	_____

EXPENSES THAT VARY DEPENDING ON YOUR LIFE-STYLE

Transportation	_____	_____	_____
Personal schooling	_____	_____	_____
Your clothing	_____	_____	_____
Children's clothing	_____	_____	_____
Meals away from home	_____	_____	_____
Entertainment	_____	_____	_____
Costs of child care	_____	_____	_____
Other	_____	_____	_____

PREPARING FOR THE FIRST DAYS AND WEEKS

You have checked out all the possible arrangements and have finally selected one. Now your child needs your support and understanding during these first days.

Before the first day, ask the staff about their policy on personal objects from home and how they want you to handle clothing, food, toys, and other personal items. If toys from home are allowed, then ask your child if he or she wants to bring a toy or other familiar item. The child's clothing should be wash and wear, easy to put on and take off, and made to take the rough and tumble of play with other children. Be sure to label each article of clothing with the child's name to make sure it does not get lost. Pack an extra pair of play pants and underwear in a bag marked with your child's name. Make sure the staff has your phone number at work and an emergency number of a friend or relative to call if for any reason you cannot be reached. Complete information should be left with the staff before you leave your child. If you have made a sincere effort to investigate the child-care situation thoroughly, when you leave your child for the first time you will be able to do so with peace of mind. You should be able to work or do whatever you have planned in full confidence. If you are relaxed and comfortable, your child will be too.

Prepare your child for the first day by talking about being at a nice new place where he or she will meet and play with other children. Mention that you will leave him there while you go to go to work. Say that the person there will know where you are all the time and can call you if necessary.

It is up to the center director or the family day-care home provider to give you permission to stay with your child the first day or as long as necessary. Ask him or her if you may bring your lunch and eat with your child that first day. Be there, but let your child find his or her own way. When the children are engaged in an activity, you may be able to assist. If for some reason you will not be able to stay for the entire day, tell your child earlier that you will be leaving and will be back later to take him or her home. If you think your child will be upset about this, arrange your schedule so you won't have to leave, or if you must leave, return as soon as possible. You may also want to leave for a few hours just to allow your child a chance to be there without you. The important thing is to make this change as smooth as possible. The staff will probably give you a lot of friendly assistance, so include them in your plans.

Sharing some of your thoughts and plans with your child the week prior to the change is important. As you are getting dressed, you can say, "Soon I will be going to work, and you'll be going to a new school where you can have a good time with some other children. We will have to get dressed and have breakfast earlier in the morning to get to the center. You'll have a chance to play with the other children, and I think you'll like it very much."

You can say as you are getting ready to go the first morning, "I'm going to take you to Mrs. Jones's house and you can play with the other children while I talk to her. Then I'll be leaving." Or you can say, "I'm going to take you there and stay with you a while. Then I'll be going to work."

Stay at the center or home at least until the teacher or provider talks directly to your child, and your child wishes to begin an activity. Sometimes this first conversation involves asking your child's name and making a nametag, or inviting your child to begin a game or join a circle of children engaged in a song or story. The important thing is to be there with the teacher's permission and your child's awareness that enough time will be given for him or her to feel totally all right before the two of you part company. Some children will move right into the group and begin to participate immediately and comfortably from the first hour. Others will benefit from their parents' sensitive watching and sharing until the strangeness and newness wears off a bit. For some it may take a day, for others a week, and for others still longer. Don't push or rush your child. Being sensitive to your child's responses at the outset will save a lot of unnecessary aggravation later.

Your child is unique and like no other at the center or home. Make sure the staff knows your child as well as possible before you leave, and that they recognize some of the subtle needs he or she has expressed to you. These needs and your own should always be respected and given attention.

Although it is best for your child's emotional well-being to make the transition to the new place gradually, this is often impossible. You may not be able to get time off from work. Or the provider you have chosen might prefer to introduce your child by him or herself. In each case, tell your child ahead of time a little about what to expect and what he or she should do. You've made a decision about your part in handling any emotional upsets that arise and are setting a positive tone. If you have fears, try not to show them. Let your child know you recognize how he or she feels and guide your child towards coping with the situation alone. No matter what your child can understand intellectually, he or she will respond to the essence of what you are saying and pick up cues from that about how to behave. If you tell children what to expect, and what they hear is positive and without fear, the transition can be simple.

BRIDGING THE GAP BETWEEN HOME AND CHILD CARE

In a child's life, a gap opens between the world at home and the world of child care. A place away from home is not home: it is a new place to learn and grow. Your child should be encouraged to enjoy this place, the new friends, and the fresh experiences. He or she also has a responsibility to participate and make the most of the experience. Remember—do not pressure your child; just reassure him or her that the new experiences will be valuable to both of you and a new adventure.

During the first few weeks adjust your schedule to make more time to be at the center or home. Let the staff know you are willing to do so as an interested and concerned parent.

Contact the other parents who live nearby to arrange car pools, informal meetings, or sitting swaps. Find out what kinds of activities parents are involved in, when the meetings are, and either join what is going on already or simply contribute whatever interests and ideas you have.

Take time each day to talk with the staff about any concerns or information they might need to know about your child. Tell them about a cold, an upset in the family, a new job, or anything else that in any way would affect your child or interfere with the day's program. You also want the staff to know that you are interested in learning about your child's progress, the activities during the day, and any new friends made.

Find out if there are activities or discussions you can undertake at home to continue the daytime activities. Focus on what happened during the day. Sometimes staff people are eager to tell you only good things about your child. Make it clear to them you're interested in how your child feels, and that you accept his or her feelings, good or bad.

Here are some suggestions for things to talk about with the staff at the end of the day:

1. What pleased my child most? What displeased my child?
2. Did my child take a nap?
3. Did my child enjoy the food? What did my child eat?
4. Is there a new food we can talk about and also have at home?
5. Did my child learn a new skill he or she wants to share?
6. Was there a special activity which could be talked about?
7. Is there a new friend to invite over to play on the weekend?
8. How are my child's relationships with other children or adults?

In this way you can keep in touch with your child's life away from you. If a problem arises, you'll have an idea where it started and be able to respond more effectively.

The staff also needs to know what is happening with your child at home. Your child may arrive with particular needs that day.

Here are some things to tell the staff at the beginning of the day:

1. What's going on at home.
2. Any physical or emotional problems.
3. A new experience your child has had.
4. What your child tells you regarding the program.
5. What changes you see in your child related to the program such as new abilities, interests, and attitudes.

Make sure to thank your child-care providers for the efforts they make on behalf of your child. They very much appreciate it. Birthdays and other special days, such as Christmas, are enhanced by small gifts.

Help your child make the transition from child care to home by talking about the things that have happened and the things he has done during the day. Listening to your child and your care providers is your way of positively connecting their day with your own.

Don't burden your child or care providers with complaints about your tough day at the office. It's understandable that you will be tired by the end of the day, and that makes it all the more important to take some time for yourself. Take a walk, find a quiet space to breathe and relax. And make sure you have someone to whom you can talk about any negative feelings. The time you spend away from your child every day is the time for you to handle your responsibilities in the world. If you can handle each part of your life in a positive way, you will make life easier for yourself and all those involved with you.

KNOWING YOUR CHILD IS HAPPY

You know your child best. You can judge with your own eyes and ears what is happening with your child as the time passes. Children usually tell the truth. If your child looks forward to going to the place each day, speaks openly about what happened during the day, brings things home that he or she drew, painted, or made, is able to sleep as usual, and seems generally secure and happy, you know you've made a good choice.

Don't panic at the first problem. There are bound to be several problems that arise in the first days. Children vary greatly in what they can adapt to and handle. If you share some of the problems with the staff or other parents, solutions usually can be found. If for any reason you see that the situation is not working out for you and your child after a few weeks, let the care giver know about the problems you are having, and start looking elsewhere for an alternative. Out of consideration, you should not leave without notifying the staff, no matter how discontented you may be.

CONNECTING WITH OTHER PARENTS

"Some of my best friends are people I met through my son's nursery school."

"She and I worked in the cooperative together and I knew we'd be friends forever."

"Come to a reunion. The kids would love to get together."

Child care is a great avenue for finding friends in a world where you may feel lonely, isolated, and distant from familiar faces. Seeing other parents and teachers interacting with children gives you perspective on what you're doing and maybe some ideas on how to do things differently. Get involved in your child-care arrangement—it's a great opportunity for you, as well as good for the children and the center or home.

If you interact with teachers, parents, and also the other children in a friendly way, or take part in some activities for the center, the whole center will seem more personal. Your friendliness will contribute to building a good feeling all around.

SOME ACTIVITIES FOR YOU

Spend a few hours at the center or home reading stories, playing games, or cooking with the children.

Contribute some new decorations for the place—curtains, pictures, or plants.

Contact other parents to organize a fund-raising event for new equipment and toys.

Invite a guest, such as a pediatrician, nurse, or community health worker to give a health talk.

Give individual attention to a child who may be in special need due to a personal problem.

Establish a sitting-swapping announcement bulletin board as one way for parents to share with each other.

Set up a revolving toy library that parents can contribute to and share in.

If space is available, set up a parent lounge or a place where parents can relax, sip coffee, and spend a few moments talking before they leave or pick up their children.

Send letters to city, state, and national officials supporting the funding of new child-care programs. Describe the value of the program you are part of and why it helps not only those involved but society at large.

PARENT DISCUSSION GROUPS

Meeting other parents for discussion in informal groups can be valuable to everyone. Just knowing that you're not alone in your problems when things are rough can ease a lot of stress.

At a party, you might feel a little ridiculous seeking out someone to talk to about "Batman and my child's problems with nightmares" while others are discussing world affairs. Parents' groups give you a chance talk about what is on your mind. It's an occasion to exchange information about what concerns you and to help other people out. Solving your child's problems with nightmares might not seem as important as world problems to you, but it is! An informal parents' group can:

1. give you the assistance you need (so that your own nightmares disappear);
2. reassure you when things don't work;
3. give you understanding and support; and
4. help you grow.

Some people find their parents' group so satisfying they wouldn't miss a single meeting. If they can't find a sitter, they bundle up the children and take them along. If they're attending a course with other parents, they want to take another course as soon as that one is over. A parents' group becomes an important part of their life-style while their children are young.

Sometimes new parents will gather informally, meeting once a week or twice a month. Some parents get together through their children's child-care arrangements. Co-ops often set aside a few nights a month for parent groups. Centers are often very responsive to parent's desires to get together. Some even provide a leader for the group who has specialized knowledge in family problems. There are usually parent groups in metropolitan areas that offer special courses on all the aspects of being a parent. These courses help you to deal with yourself and your problems, as well as your relationship to society.

SHARING EXPERIENCES

Parenthood and work are a difficult combination. The stresses can overwhelm anyone at times. We often are like jugglers with too many roles or balls in the air—finances, home maintenance, food, our children's changing needs, personal needs, just to name a few. Like experienced jugglers, we need balance, efficiency, timing, and experience.

Comparing and Choosing | 93

The more successful you are with the life-style you choose, the more competent you are likely to be at making arrangements and scheduling, getting things done, being true to yourself, and enjoying your children. These are all things you get better at as you gain experience. Your ability grows and changes.

The amount of time you spend with your child is important, but the way that time is spent is more important. Studies of working mothers versus nonworking mothers show that the most important factor in children's emotional well-being (and later functioning in society), is the quality of the relationship among the mother, father, and child rather than the quantity or amount of time spent together.

You took a step to balance the elements of a busy and balanced life when you figured out your essential goals and priorities.

Now that you know where you're at, you can begin to schedule your time and establish a new routine. You need sufficient time for each of the following:

1. Maintaining your home
2. Pursuing personal goals
3. Teaching and enjoying your children
4. Learning from them
5. Reaching out to people
6. Spending time alone

Probably it seems there's not quite enough of you to go around, with all the responsibilities you're juggling. Remember: these can be handled one at a time. You can't do it all at once; you can't talk to your child, settle a fight, clean house, figure out your finances, calculate your menu for a week, plan the most efficient shopping route, socialize with friends, and make a phone call all at the same time, though you have probably found yourself trying to. You can become harried, and "harried" quickly becomes "nasty." To avoid this you have to take all the time you need and handle each problem as it comes along. Don't try to be "Supermom" and lose your sense of humor and balance under the strain of responsibility.

To take care of your multiple responsibilities requires efficiency and skill, as does any other difficult job. You will gain those skills in time. Budget time for relaxing, personal enjoyment and growth, nurturing your children, and cultivating friendships, as well as for household routines and work. Long hours of work should be balanced against time for yourself. You need to find ways to relax and share your feelings.

Stick to what's most important to you. The world is seldom the way you would like it to be, so don't waste energy on complaining or worrying. Put your energy into something useful, like supporting the creation of expanded and improved child-care services in your community. Find out to whom you should write to support child-care legislation, and then write a few letters (and keep writing). Better yet, become active. Organize a parent participation group or work with your local child-care advocacy organizations.

Find some form of relaxation, though you want to make sure that it is not a form of escape from the problems in your life. And make room for the ups and downs of life. Some days will work better than others.

You can't *do* everything and can't *be* everything to *all* people at *all* times. Don't feel guilty! Catch yourself when you worry about your child at work, or about your work and your responsibilities when you are at home. You can overcome some of your fears by sharing your feelings with other people who have the same interests and concerns. If you find the stresses in your life overwhelming you, get help in working things out through counseling.

If you pursue your own needs and interests to the extent that your child feels left out, uncared for, unimportant, or insecure about what to expect, his or her needs accelerate. Soon you'll find your child making you both miserable.

Neither you nor your child need be miserable. If you interact with your child in a gentle, friendly, giving way, you will bring joy to both of you. Remember how it is to be a child: children like to be treated pleasantly and with respect. They don't want to feel threatened. Communicate about your feelings directly and allow your child to share his or her feelings with you. You will both stand to gain.

Here are a few suggestions:

1. *Create special times.* Spend time with your child regularly, both scheduled and spontaneous. During these times allow no inter-

ruptions; make your child feel important. Get to know what is happening to your child. Focus on his or her needs. If your child feels confident that he or she is loved, you will feel a lot less guilty about not being around all the time.

2. *Simplify living.* Have potluck suppers and share cooking and sitting with other parents as a regular part of your life. Make clean up something everyone in the family contributes to, according to their ability.

3. *Expand your horizons.* Take a course; better yet, take two courses—one for yourself, one to share with your children. Work toward a goal—get that better job, work on something such as a community improvement project that will benefit others, and so on. Express yourself. Find a little time to do what you like to do best.

4. *Support yourself emotionally.* Don't let yourself be argued out of expressing how you feel or what you want. Don't be afraid to ask others, including children and friends, to work as hard as you do.

5. *Take time off.* Do things alone once in a while. Take time for your personal health, physical, and emotional needs.

A FINAL WORD ON CHILD CARE AND YOU AS A WORKING PARENT

Child-care services can be as good as we want them to be if we are willing to work for, create, and improve them. Perhaps at some future date the amount of money and resources available will be adequate to provide the necessary physical environments and optimal educational and social services for every child. Until then we must work together to improve child care. The suggestions in this guide point the way toward some of the kinds of services that should ideally be part of every child-care program now.

As you seek to balance all the roles you have to perform, I wish you well. When you run into difficulty, remember that so many of us want to reach the same goals. You have lots of company and support. Don't be shy about asking for assistance. Everyone needs it at one time or another, in one form or another. Who knows? Perhaps you will find a child-care situation that is perfect for everyone concerned. I certainly hope so.

Please share this guide with a friend and write and let me know your experiences with *Choosing Child Care*. I hope it has been a useful guide to you and your friends, and I hope your child has the best child-care arrangement possible at this time.

APPENDIX: Resources

CHILD-CARE AGENCIES AND ORGANIZATIONS

These organizations are sources for additional information and assistance regarding child care and parenting. To find out what they have to offer write them directly:

American Home Economics Education Association, Inc.
2010 Massachusetts Avenue, N.W.
Washington, D.C. 20036

American Parents Committee, Inc.
1346 Connecticut Avenue, N.W.
Washington, D.C. 20036

American Red Cross
Director, Nursing and Health Services
17th and D Streets, N.W.
Washington, D.C. 20006

Association for Childhood Education International, Inc.
3615 Wisconsin Avenue, N.W.
Washington, D.C. 20016

Child Development Associate Consortium, Inc.
805 Fifteenth Street, N.W.
Washington, D.C. 20005

Children's Defense Fund, Inc.
1520 New Hampshire Avenue, N.W.
Washington, D.C. 20036

Coalition for Children and Youth, Inc.
815 Fifteenth Street, N.W.
Washington, D.C. 20005

Day Care Council of America, Inc.
805 Fifteenth Street, N.W.
Washington, D.C. 20005

Family Impact Seminar
1001 Connecticut Avenue, N.W.,
Suite 732
Washington, D.C. 20036

National Association for Child Development and Education, Inc.
1834 Connecticut Avenue, N.W.
Washington, D.C. 20009

National Committee for Citizens in Education
410 Wilde Lake Village Green
Columbia, Maryland 21044

National Committee on Household Employment, Inc.
7705 Georgia Avenue, N.W.
Washington, D.C. 20012

National Council of State Committees for Children and Youth
1614 Garfield
Laramie, Wyoming 82070

National Organization for Women
Task Force on Child Care
45 Newberry Street
Boston, Massachusetts 02116

National Parents Federation for Day Care and Child Development, Inc.
429 Lewis Street
Somerset, New Jersey 08893

The Non-Sexist Child Development Project
Women's Action Alliance
370 Lexington Avenue
New York, New York 10017

Organization Mondiale Pour Education Pr'escolaire
(O.M.E.P. World Organization for Early Childhood)

1319 Denby Road
Baltimore, Maryland 21204
(Sponsors International Year of the Child)

ETHNIC AND OTHER SPECIAL ORGANIZATIONS

For information regarding bilingual, ethnic, religious, and other types of specialized child care, write to:

American Montessori Society (AMS)
150 Fifth Avenue
New York, New York 10011

Aspira of America, Inc.
Research Division
11800 Sunrise Valley Drive
Reston, Virginia 22091

East Coast Migrant Head Start Projects
1234 Massachusetts Avenue, N.W., Room 823
Washington, D.C. 20003

Lutheran Church—Missouri Synod
Board of Parish Education
3358 South Jefferson Avenue
St. Louis, Missouri 63118

National Black Child Development Institute, Inc.
1463 Rhode Island Avenue, N.W.
Washington, D.C. 20005

National Black Parents Organization
P.O. 6519
Washington, D.C. 20009

National Clearinghouse for Bilingual Education
InterAmerica Research Associates, Inc.
1500 Wilson Boulevard, Suite 802
Rosslyn, Virginia 22209
Hotline 1-800-336-4560

National Conference of Catholic Charities
1346 Connecticut Avenue, N.W.
Washington, D.C. 20036

National Council for Black Child Development, Inc.
P.O. Box 28353
Washington, D.C. 20005

National Council of Jewish Women
15 East 26th Street
New York, New York 10010

National Council of La Raza
1725 I Street, N.W., 2nd Floor
Washington, D.C. 20005

National Council of Negro Women, Inc.
1346 Connecticut Avenue, N.W.
Washington, D.C. 20036

National Indian Education Association
1115 Second Avenue South
Minneapolis, Minnesota 55403

National Jewish Welfare Board
Program Development Department
15 East 26th Street
New York, New York 10010

Parent Cooperative Preschools International
14912 Rocking Spring Drive
Rockville, Maryland 20853

Save The Children
48 Wilton Road
Westport, Connecticut 06880

United Church of Christ—Board for Homeland Ministries
Division of Health and Welfare
Child Care Resource Center
132 West 31st Street
New York, New York 10001

United Methodist Church, Board of Global Ministries Division
Health and Welfare Ministries Division
1200 Davis Street
Evanston, Illinois 60201

United Presbyterian Church in the U.S.A.
Association for Welfare Organizational Relations
475 Riverside Drive
New York, New York 10027

FEDERAL AGENCIES SUPPORTING DAY CARE

For information about federally supported child-care programs and other federal activities, write to the following agencies for current information:

Administration for Native American Programs
Department of Health, Education, and Welfare
200 Independence Avenue, S.W.
Washington, D.C. 20242

Department of Agriculture, Administrator
Science and Education Extension (SEA—Extension)
Washington, D.C. 20250

Department of Agriculture, Director, Child Nutrition Division
Food and Nutrition Service
Washington, D.C. 20250

Appalachian Regional Commission
1666 Connecticut Avenue, N.W.
Washington, D.C. 20235

Bureau of Indian Affairs
Department of the Interior
1951 Constitution Avenue, S.W.
Washington, D.C. 20242

CETA—Comprehensive Employment and Training Administration
Department of Health, Education, and Welfare
7th and D Streets, S.W., Room 5008
Washington, D.C. 20202

CETA
Department of Labor
601 D Street, N.W.
Washington, D.C. 20213

Community Services Administration
Office of Public Affairs
1200 Nineteenth Street, N.W.
Washington, D.C. 20506

Cooperative Extension Service
U.S. Department of Agriculture
(Offices located in Land Grant Universities in the 50 states, the District of Columbia, Guam, Puerto Rico, and the Virgin Islands; in the sixteen 1890 colleges in the United States; and at Tuskegee Institute, Tuskegee, Alabama)

Day Care Division
Administration for Children, Youth and Families
U.S. Department of Health, Education, and Welfare
P.O. Box 1182
Washington, D.C. 20013

Division of Education Services
Bureau of Education for the Handicapped
Handicapped Preschool and School Program
U.S. Office of Education
Washington, D.C. 20013

Department of Education
400 Maryland Avenue, S.W.
Washington, D.C. 20202

Head Start
U.S. Department of Health, Education, and Welfare
P.O. Box 1182
Washington, D.C. 20013

Housing and Urban Development
Department of Community Development Block Grant Program
451 Seventh Street, S.W.
Washington, D.C. 20410

Department of Labor, Women's Bureau
200 Constitution Avenue, N.W.
Washington, D.C. 20210

Migrant Programs (Education)
FOB-6
400 Maryland Avenue, S.W., Room 2031
Washington, D.C. 20202

Migrant Programs (Health)
Parklawn
5600 Fisher Lane
Rockville, Maryland 20857

Title IV-A
(Aid to Families with Dependent Children)
Office of Family Assistance
Department of Health, Education, and Welfare
Switzer Building, 330 C Street, S.W., Room 4110
Washington, D.C. 20201

Work Incentive Program
Department of Labor
601 D Street, N.W., Room 5100
Washington, D.C. 20213

STATE DAY CARE AGENCIES

For information on child-care licensing in your state, you can contact the appropriate office listed below. Write ahead for information about available child-care services if you are planning to relocate to another state.

Alabama
Supervisor of Child Caring Institutions and Agencies
State Department of Pensions and Security
64 North Union Street
Montgomery, Alabama 36130

Alaska
Department of Health and Social Services
Pouch H-05
Juneau, Alaska 99811

Arizona
Child Day Care Health Consultant
Arizona State Department of Health
1624 West Adams Street
Phoenix, Arizona 85007

Arkansas
Day Care Specialist
Department of Human Services
P.O. Box 1437
Little Rock, Arkansas 72203

California
Department of Social Services
744 P Street
Mail Station 19-50
Sacramento, California 95814

Colorado
State of Colorado
Department of Social Services
1515 Sherman Street
Denver, Colorado 80203

Connecticut
Day Care Licensing
Connecticut State Department of Health
79 Elm Street
Hartford, Connecticut 06115

Delaware
Chief, Day Care Licensing
Bureau of Child Development
P.O. Box 309
Wilmington, Delaware 19899

District of Columbia
Department of Human Resources
Licensing Certification Division
1406 L Street, N.W.
Washington, D.C. 20005

Florida
Department of Health and Rehabilitative Services
1317 Winewood Boulevard
Tallahassee, Florida 32301

Georgia
Child Care Licensing Unit
618 Ponce de Leon Avenue
Atlanta, Georgia 30308

Hawaii
State Department of Social Services and Housing
Day Care Licensing Unit
Public Welfare Division
1319 Miller Street
Honolulu, Hawaii 96813

Idaho
Day Care Licensing
State of Idaho
Department of Health and Welfare
Statehouse
Boise, Idaho 83720

Illinois
Day Care Licensing
Department of Children and Family Services
1 North Old State Capitol Plaza
Springfield, Illinois 62706

Indiana
Day Care Supervisor
Indiana State Department of Public Welfare
141 South Meridian Street, 6th floor
Indianapolis, Indiana 46225

Iowa
Day Care Supervisor
Department of Social Services
Lucas State Office Building
Des Moines, Iowa 50319

Kansas
Day Care Supervisor
Department of Social and Rehabilitation Services
State Office Building
Topeka, Kansas 66612

Kentucky
Department of Human Resources
Bureau for Social Services
275 East Main Street
Frankfort, Kentucky 40621

Lousiana
Department of Health and Human Resources
Office of Licensing and Regulation

Office of the Assistant Secretary
P.O. Box 3767
Baton Rouge, Lousiana 70821

Maine
State of Maine
Department of Human Services
Statehouse
Augusta, Maine 04333

Maryland
Child Day Care Center Coordinator
State Department of Health and Mental Hygiene
201 West Preston Street
Baltimore, Maryland 21201

Massachusetts
Office for Children
Director of Day Care Licensing
120 Boylston Street
Boston, Massachusetts 02116

Michigan
Department of Social Services
300 South Capitol Avenue
Lansing, Michigan 49926

Minnesota
Department of Public Welfare
Licensing Division
Centennial Office Building
St. Paul, Minnesota 55155

Mississippi
Day Care Supervisor
Division of Family and Children's Services
P.O. Box 4321
Fondren Station
Jackson, Mississippi 39216

Missouri
Missouri Department of Social Services
Division of Family Services
Broadway State Office Building
P.O. Box 88
Jefferson City, Missouri 65103

Montana
Social and Rehabilitation Services
P.O. Box 4210
Helena, Montana 59601

Nebraska
Day Care Welfare Consultant
Department of Public Welfare
P.O. Box 95026
Lincoln, Nebraska 68509

Nevada
State Department of Health
Department of Human Resources
505 East King Street
Carson City, Nevada 89710

New Hampshire
Day Care Licensing
Division of Welfare
Concord, New Hampshire 03301

New Jersey
Division of Youth and Family Services
Bureau of Licensing
1 South Montgomery Street, #400
Trenton, New Jersey 08625

New Mexico
Child Care Licensing
725 St. Michael's Drive
P.O. Box 968
Santa Fe, New Mexico 87503

New York
Division of Day Care
New York City Health Department
350 Broadway
New York, New York 10013

North Carolina
Office of Child Day Care Licensing
Department of Social Services
P.O. Box 10157
Raleigh, North Carolina 27602

North Dakota
Supervisor of Children and Family Day Care Services

State Capitol Building
15th Floor
Bismarck, North Dakota 58501

Ohio
Department of Public Welfare
Division of Social Services
30 East Broad Street
30th Floor
Columbus, Ohio 43215

Oklahoma
Children's Day Care Services
State Department of Public Welfare
P.O. Box 25352
Oklahoma City, Oklahoma 73125

Oregon
Department of Human Resources
Children's Service Division
198 Commercial Street, S.E.
Salem, Oregon 97310

Pennsylvania
Licensing Supervisor
Children and Youth
1514 North Second Street
Harrisburg, Pennsylvania 17102

Puerto Rico
Puerto Rico Department of Social Services
P.O. Box 11697
Santurce, Puerto Rico 00908

Rhode Island
Department of Social and Rehabilitative Services
Division of Community Services, Child Welfare
610 Mt. Pleasant
Providence, Rhode Island 02908

South Carolina
South Carolina Department of Social Services
P.O. Box 1520
Columbia, South Carolina 29202

South Dakota
Department of Social Services
Illinois Street
Kniep Building
Pierre, South Dakota 57501

Tennessee
Day Care Licensing
Department of Public Welfare
State Office Building
Nashville, Tennessee 37219

Texas
State Department of Public Welfare
105 Riverside Drive
Austin, Texas 78704

Utah
State of Utah
Department of Social Services
Division of Family Services
150 West North Temple, Room 370
P.O. Box 2500
Salt Lake City, Utah 84110

Vermont
Department of Social and Rehabilitation Services
Licensing and Regulations Unit
State Office Building
Montpelier, Vermont 05602

Virginia
Division of Licensing
8007 Discovery Drive
Richmond, Virginia 23288

Virgin Islands
Department of Social Welfare
P.O. Box 539, Charlotte Amalie
St. Thomas, Virgin Islands 00801

Washington
Bureau of Children's Services
Licensing Program
Department of Social and Health Services
Mail Stop OB-2, 41-D
Olympia, Washington 98504

West Virginia
Day Care Unit
State Department of Welfare
1900 Washington Street, E.
Charleston, West Virginia 25305

Wisconsin
Department of Health and Social Services
1 West Wilson Street, Room 384
Madison, Wisconsin 53702

Wyoming
Day Care Supervisor
Division of Public Assistance
State Office Building
Cheyenne, Wyoming 82002

CHILD-CARE INFORMATION FOR CHILDREN WITH SPECIAL CONDITIONS

Your child may need special care as a result of a physical, emotional, mental, or learning disability. Because some child-care settings are not equipped to provide such care, you may have to spend extra time and effort selecting an arrangement. The following organizations and government agencies may be able to provide information about child care for children with special needs.

STATE AGENCIES FOR CHILDREN WITH HANDICAPPING CONDITIONS

Most states have departments with titles similar to those listed below. Call your state welfare department for specific names of departments, telephone numbers, and addresses:

City or County Superintendent of Schools
Health Department—Maternal Child Clinics
Education Department—Division of Special Education
Departments of Mental Health and Mental Retardation Clinics

FEDERAL AGENCIES FOR CHILDREN WITH HANDICAPPING CONDITIONS

The following federal agencies may also be of help:

Administration for Children, Youth and Families
Head Start, Child Care Services
P.O. Box 1182
Washington, D.C. 20013

Bureau of Education for the Handicapped
OE-BEH Donohoe Building
400 Maryland Avenue, S.W.
Washington, D.C. 20202

Department of Health, Education, and Welfare

Rehabilitation Services Administration
Office of Public Affairs
330 C Street, S.W., #1427
Washington, D.C. 20207

Health Services Administration
5600 Fishers Lane
Rockville, Maryland 20852

National Institute of Mental Health
5600 Fishers Lane
Rockville, Maryland 20852

NATIONAL ORGANIZATIONS FOR CHILDREN WITH HANDICAPPING CONDITIONS

The following organizations provide informational services to families with special needs. If you need help look for the names of the organizations listed below in your telephone directory or call the social welfare department of your city or county.

Alexander Graham Bell Association for the Deaf
3417 Volta Place, N.W.
Washington, D.C. 20007

American Association on Mental Deficiency
5101 Wisconsin Avenue, N.W.
Washington, D.C. 20007

American Foundation for the Blind
15 West 11th Street
New York, New York 10017

Association for Children with Learning Disabilities
4156 Library Road
Pittsburgh, Pennsylvania 15234

Association for Retarded Citizens, Inc.
405 Riggs Road, N.E.
Washington, D.C. 20011

Closer Look Information Center
P.O. Box 1492
Washington, D.C. 20013

Council for Exceptional Children
1920 Association Drive
Reston, Virginia 22091

Cystic Fibrosis Foundation
6000 Executive Boulevard, Suite 309
Rockville, Maryland 20852

Epilepsy Foundation of America
1828 L Street, N.W.
Washington, D.C. 20036

Mental Health Association
1800 North Kent Street
Arlington, Virginia 22209

Muscular Dystrophy Associations of America
810 Seventh Avenue
New York, New York 10019

National Easter Seal Society
2023 West Ogden Avenue
Chicago, Illinois 60612

National Foundation—March of Dimes Headquarters
P.O. Box 2000
White Plains, New York 10605

National Society for Autistic Children
169 Tampa Avenue
Albany, New York 12208

United Cerebral Palsy Association, Inc.
66 East 34th Street
New York, New York 10016

SINGLE PARENTS/PARENTS GROUPS

Single parents and other parents who want advice and assistance may find the following resources helpful:

Big Brothers/Sisters of America
220 Suburban Station Building
Philadelphia, Pennsylvania 19103
(Check your telephone directory for local chapters.)

Boys' and Girls' Clubs of America
771 First Avenue
New York, New York 10017
(Check your telephone directory for local chapters.)

Children's hospitals

Churches, synagogues, temples, church clubs, community centers

Local self-help groups, chapters of national women's organizations, child care advocacy groups

Local Y groups such as YWCA, YMCA, YWHA, and YMHA

Momma: A Magazine for Single Mothers
P.O. Box 567
Venice, California 90291

Parent-teacher associations

Parents without Partners
7910 Woodmont Avenue
Washington, D.C. 20014
(This organization has local chapters throughout the country that deal with the needs of single parents.)

Social Services agencies, Red Cross chapters

YMCA—Circular #6
291 Broadway
New York, New York 10007
(This circular provides a listing of single parent groups in the United States.)

CHILD ABUSE AND NEGLECT AND CRISIS INTERVENTION

Child abuse can occur in various personal situations. The forms may range from child neglect to physical abuse. If you need help to deal with this stress, seek it immediately. If you suspect that a care giver might be abusing your child, contact your local welfare or social services office to report the problem.

Sometimes during family emergencies or crises, children can be placed in facilities offering special temporary 24-hour care. These services are called: "emergency", "crisis", or "respite" care and are used when families have problems that might lead to the abuse or neglect of the children; if parents suddenly need emergency hospital care; or when parents need a rest from the strain of caring for a child with a handicapping condition. To find out whether such care is available in your area, contact your local public health department or social services or welfare department.

Some resources to help you are:

National Center on Child Abuse and Neglect
U.S. Department of Health, Education, and Welfare

Administration for Children, Youth, and Families
P.O. Box 1182
Washington, D.C. 20013

Parents Anonymous
22330 Hawthorne Boulevard, #208
Torrence, California 90505
(This is a national self-help parents' organization, with local chapters throughout the U.S. The toll-free number is 1-800-421-0353.)

SUGGESTED EQUIPMENT
for Preschool Child-Care Programs

OUTDOOR EQUIPMENT

PLAY

balls swings
ladders tricycles
sawhorses wagons
slides wheelbarrows

SAND PLAY

collections of cars, boats, etc.
hose
large plastic dishpans or tubs
large, smooth tin cans, pots and pans
pails
sandbox
shovels, scoops, or spoons
sifting screens
small dishes (metal or plastic)
sprinkling cans
straws and paper cups
wading pool

CARPENTRY

hammers
nails with large heads
saws
soft pieces of wood

GARDENING

flower pots
plot of ground
seeds
sprinkling cans
trowels

INDOOR EQUIPMENT

PLAY

>barrel to climb through
>punching bag
>steps and platform

BLOCK BUILDING

>assorted wooden blocks
>large blocks for storage

HOUSEKEEPING

>brooms and dustpans
>chests for keeping equipment
>clothesline and clothespins
>cooking utensils
>dishes
>dolls
>doll beds
>doll carriages
>empty food cartons
>ironing board and iron
>play clothes
>play furniture
>remnants and pieces for costumes
>telephones that dial
>washtubs and washboards

MANIPULATIVE PLAY

>dominoes
>handlooms and wool
>needles with large eyes
>nested blocks
>pegboards
>puzzles
>remnants of material
>spindles of blocks
>thread or colored yarn
>wooden beads or macaroni and strings

MUSIC

- bells
- cymbals
- drums
- music books
- record player
- records
- rhythm sticks
- tambourines
- triangles

CRAFT ACTIVITIES

- blunt scissors, paper, and wastebaskets
- bulletin board or clothesline and clothespins for display of paintings
- colored modeling dough
- finger paints
- jumbo crayons in individual boxes
- newsprint
- plain paper, construction paper, paste
- shelf paper for finger painting
- small jars

FURNISHINGS

- chairs, one for each child
- clock
- colorful window shades
- cots with washable covers and light blankets
- dishes and equipment for meals
- fire extinguishers
- first-aid supplies
- mirrors
- mops, pails, brooms, dustpans, dusting and cleaning cloths
- needles, thread, safety pins
- paper towels
- pictures, plants
- file folders
- Scotch tape
- screens or low movable shelves to separate quiet from play areas
- small tables with washable tops
- soap
- storage for supplies
- thumbtacks
- toilet paper
- wastebasket

FURTHER READING

CHILD CARE

Babysitter, DHEW Publication AHAD, 74–45. Washington, D.C.: U.S. Government Printing Office, 1979. $.70.

Babysitting: a Concise Guide. New York: Archway Paperback Pocketbooks, 1972. $1.50.

BROAD, LAURA, and BUTTERWORTH, NANCY. *The Playgroup Handbook.* New York: St. Martin's Press, 1974. 306 pp. $5.95.

Child Care and Disabled Dependent Care. IRS Publication #503. Washington, D.C.: Internal Revenue Service. Free.

Day Care and Early Education: The Magazine. New York: Human Sciences Press.

League of Women Voters Education Fund, Publication 281. *Day Care: Who Needs It?* Washington, D.C.: League of Women Voters Education Fund, 1973. Free.

Metropolitan Life Insurance Company. *Day Care: What and Why.* New York: Metropolitan Life Insurance Co., 1972. Free.

Metropolitan Life Insurance Company. *Mothers at Work.* New York: Metropolitan Insurance Co., 1973. 14 pp. Free.

Metropolitan Life Insurance Company. *Sitting Safely for Babysitters.* New York: Metropolitan Life Insurance Co., 1976. 15 pp. Free.

National Association for the Education of Young Children. *Some Ways of Distinguishing a Good School or Center for Young Children.* Washington, D.C.: National Association for the Education of Young Children. $1.00.

Office of Human Development, U.S. Department of Health, Education, and Welfare. *Day Care for Your Children.* Washington, D.C.: U.S. Government Printing Office, 1974. Free.

ADVICE AND SUPPORT FOR WORKING PARENTS

AUERBACH, STEVANNE, *Confronting the Child Care Crisis*, Boston: Beacon Press, 1979.

———. *The Whole Child: A Sourcebook.* New York: G. P. Putnam's Sons, 1981.

BENJAMIN, LOIS. *So You Want to Become a Working Mother!* New York: McGraw-Hill Book Co., 1968. Paper. New York: Funk & Wagnalls, 1966.

BIRD, CAROLINE. *The Two-Paycheck Marriage: How Women At Work Are Changing Life in America.* New York: Rawson, Wade Publishers, 1979.

BRIETBART, VICKI. *The Day Care Book.* New York: Alfred A. Knopf, 1974.

CURTIS, JEAN. *Working Mothers.* New York: Doubleday & Co., 1976.

GALINSKY, ELLEN, and HOOKS, WILLIAM. *The New Extended Family: Day Care That Works*. Boston: Houghton-Mifflin, 1977.

GREEN, MAUREEN. *Fathering*. New York: McGraw-Hill Book Co., 1976.

KLEIN, CAROLE. *The Single Parent Experience*. New York: Walker, 1973.

LEVINE, JAMES A. *Who Will Have the Children? New Options for Fathers (and Mothers)*. Philadelphia: J. B. Lippincott, 1976.

NORRIS, GLORIA, and MILLER, JOANN. *The Working Mother's Complete Handbook*. New York: E. P. Dutton, 1979.

ROBY, PAMELA. *Child Care—Who Cares?* New York: Basic Books, 1973.

SKELSEY, ALICE. *The Working Mother's Guide to Her Home, Her Family, and Herself*. New York: Random House, 1970.

STEINBERG, DAVID. *Father Journal: Five Years to Awakening to Fatherhood*. New York: Monthly Review Press, 1977.

WOOLLEY, PERSIA. *Creative Survival for Single Mothers*. Millbrae, Calif.: Celestial Arts, 1975.

INDEX

academic skills, 3
acknowledgment of child, 71, 66
activities, 34, 61, 64, 66
   for parents, 91
adapting to child care, 10
advantages of child care, 3
after-school care, 55, 60, 63–64
age difference, 22
agencies, 97–107
alternatives, 20–23, 27, 64, 84
appendix, 97

baby care, 12, 19, 34, 38, 39, 63
   what to look for, 63
baby-sitting cooperatives, 4, 20, 22, 23, 26, 84, 92
balance for children, 32, 66
   for parents, 92–95
bilingual centers, 11, 98
   for parents, 35
budget plan, 82, 83–85

centers
   acknowledgment of child, 66
   activities, 34, 61, 66
   care giver ratio, 41, 60, 61
   checklists, 67–68
   college centers, 60
   contracts, 62
   drop in, 61
   education, 66
   environment, 64
   food, 32, 33, 35, 65
   health, 65
   hospital, 61
   illness, 65
   information to give to center, 62
   licensing, 34
   mealtime, 36
   nutrition, 65
   outdoor play, 67
   programs, 32–33, 34, 35
   rest, 65
   safety features, 67, 70
   school centers, 61
   staff, 34–36, 37–43, 61, 71
   state subsidized, 60
   toilet training, 65
   toys, 65, 66
   visiting, 61, 71, 72
checklists, 69–77
   centers, 67–68
   commitment to, 79
   emotional climate, 71, 73–74
   family day-care homes, 56–57
   learning climate, 71, 75–76
   physical facility, 70, 72–73
   rating, 77–79
   social climate, 71, 76–77
child abuse, 106

child care, 1-3
  advantages, 3-4, 9
  centers, 10, 19-20, 26, 59-68
  choices, 6-13, 16, 81-96
    effects of working, 7
    family stability, 8
    know your child, 8-9
    satisfaction, 7
  community involvement, 42, 43
  consistency in child care, 12, 16
  cooperative child care, 4, 20, 22, 23, 26, 84, 92
  costs of child care, 16, 17, 55, 82, 83-85
  disadvantages, 3
  employer supported, 4, 20, 60
  family, friends, 23, 46
  good child care, 31-36
  information and referral, 26, 99
  national trends, 2
  needs of children, 8, 87
  needs of parents, 2
  preparing for first days, 85
  sources, 27, 97-107
  union, 4
child-care givers, 37-43
  disabled children and, 64
  health standards, 40
  infants and, 63
  male, 40
  parents and, 71
  personal characteristics, 52
  points to look for, 38, 39, 52-53, 70
  ratios, 41, 61
  sitters, 10, 16, 17-18, 22, 27, 32, 45-49
  teen-agers, 47
clothing for children, 86
comparing and choosing, 81-96
  activities for parents, 91
  bridging the gap, 88
  budget, 83
  discussion groups, 91
  happiness of child, 90
  other parents, 91
  preparing, 85
  sharing experiences, 92
contracts for day-care centers, 62
crisis intervention, 106
cultural identity, 11

day care
  family home, 10, 12, 16, 18, 26, 27, 51-57, 63
  large centers, 10, 16, 19-20
  sitter, 10, 16, 17-18, 22, 27, 32, 45-49, 63, 84
disabled child, 61, 64
  agencies, 104-105
  care givers for, 64
disadvantages of child care, 3
discipline, 40
discussion groups, 4, 91
divorced parents, children of, 4
drop-in child care, 61

education
  in centers, 66
  of staff, 41
effects of working, 6-13
  family stability, 8
  on the child, 8
  satisfaction, 7
employer-provided child care, 4, 20, 60
environment
  in centers, 65
  in homes, 53
equipment, 108-110
ethnic organizations, 98
evening care, 20

family
  child care and, 23, 46
  stability, 38
family day-care homes, 10, 12, 16, 18, 26, 27, 51-57, 63
  advantages, 19
  adult-child ratio, 41
  after-school care, 64
  checklist, 56-57
  disadvantages, 19
  environment, 53
  federal requirements, 53
  follow-up, 55
  health standards, 18
  information by telephone, 52
  licensing, 18
  specifics to look for, 54
  visiting, 52
federal agencies, 99

Index

federal requirements for home day care, 53
feelings, 11, 26
fitting in, 10
food, 3, 32, 33, 35, 65
  in centers, 65
friends, for child care, 23, 46

getting ready, 25
good child care, 31–36
growth patterns, 8–9

half-day programs, 22
handicapped children, 61, 64
  agencies, 104–105
Head Start, 22
health standards
  care givers, 40
  centers, 65
  family day-care homes, 18
homes, family day care, 10, 12, 16, 18, 26, 27, 51–57, 63
  advantages, 19
  after-school care, 64
  checklist, 56–57
  disadvantages, 19
  environment, 53
  federal requirements, 53
  follow-up, 55
  health standards, 18
  information gathering, 52
  licensing, 18
  ratio of adult to child, 41
  specifics to look for, 54
  visiting, 52

ill child, 19, 54
  in centers, 65
immunizations, 62
independence, child's, 3, 63
individual attention for child, 10
indoor play, 32, 66, 111
infant care, 19, 34, 63
  what to look for, 63
information and referral, 26, 97–111
information by telephone, 26, 52
information required by centers, 62
Institute for Childhood Resources, viii

kindergarten, 19, 63
knowing your child, 9–11

language
  bilingual centers, 11
  ethnic organizations, 98
  primary language of parents, 35
large groups of children, 19, 60
learning climate checklist, 71, 75–76
licensed centers, 34
licensed family day-care homes, 18, 26

male staff, 3, 40
mealtime in child-care centers, 36
mothers
  teen-age, 42–43
  working, 3, 7, 8, 84, 92, 111

naps, 33, 65
national trends in child care, 2
needs of children, 8, 87
  choosing child care, 82
  continuity, 8
  growth patterns, 8–9
  new skills, 9, 12, 13, 33, 66
needs of parents, 2, 94, 95
nurses, 20
nutrition in centers, 65

observing, 71
older child, care of, 12, 19, 34
organizations, child care, 97–107
organizing child-care information, 27
other parents, 90
outdoor play, 32, 67, 108
outgoing child, 9

parents
  cooperatives, 4, 20, 22, 23, 26, 84, 92
  discussion groups, 91, 92
  other parents, 90
  single-parents groups, 105–106
  working, 84, 92, 111
part-day programs, 22
personality, child's, 9
physical facility checklist, 73
play group, 20, 21, 26
  disadvantages, 21
pooling resources, 22
preparing for first days, 85, 86
preschools, 26
preschoolers, 19, 22, 32, 39
primary grades, 19

problems in child care, 90
programs
   disabled children, 64
   educational aspects, 66
   federal guidelines, 34–35
   observations, 61
   typical, 32
psychologists, 41, 42

quality child care, 32, 34–36, 40, 66
quality in centers, 64–67
quiet child, 9

ratios, adult to child, 41
   in centers, 61
reading about child care, 111
references, 111
referrals, 26–27, 97–111
regulations for family day care, 18, 53
resources, 97–111
responsibility in children, 8
rest, 33
   in centers, 65
return to work, 12

safety features in centers, 67, 70
school
   after-school care, 55, 60, 63–64
   before-school care, 60
   child care, 61
searching for child care, 26, 97–107
senior citizens, 41
separation, 13
sex roles, 3
sick children, 19, 54, 65
single parents' groups, 105–106
sitters, 10, 16, 17–18, 22, 27, 32, 45–49, 63, 84
   drawbacks, 46
   follow-up, 47
   instructions, 48
   interviewing, 46
   reasons for having, 46
   references, 48
   relationship to parents, 48, 49, 71
   teen-agers, 47
   terms for employment, 47
skills, childrens', 3, 9, 12, 13, 33, 66
   academic, 3
   self-help, 9, 12
small groups of children, 19, 61
social climate checklist, 71, 76–77
social workers, 41
sources for child care, 27, 97–107
special conditions, 98
special organizations, 104–105
specialists, 64
staff, 34–43, 61
   parents and, 71
   questions for, 89
   senior citizens, 41
   training and education, 41
   volunteers, 41
state
   agencies, 100–104
   licensing, 18, 53
   subsidized child-care centers, 60

talking with care givers, 27–29
   questions to ask, 28, 89
talking with your child, 86, 87
teen-age sitters, 47
time, 93
   management, 94–95
toilet training, 10
   in centers, 65
toys in centers, 65, 66, 71, 85
transition, 9, 10, 85, 86, 88, 89

university child-care centers, 60

values, parents', 11
visiting child-care providers, 61, 70, 71, 72, 82

welfare, 4
working
   effects of, 7
   mothers, 3
   parents, 84, 92, 95, 96, 111